Gnosis

Christoph Markschies

GNOSIS

An Introduction

Translated by John Bowden

T&T CLARK
A Continuum imprint
LONDON • NEW YORK

T&T CLARK LTD

A Continuum imprint

The Tower Building
11 York Road
London SE1 7NX

370 Lexington Avenue
New York 10017–6503
USA

www.continuumbooks.com

Authorized English translation of Christoph Markschies, *Die Gnosis*, published 2001 by Verlag C. H. Beck, Munich, with additions by the author.

First published 2003

ISBN 0–5670–8944–4 (hardback)
ISBN 0–5670–8945–2 (paperback)

British Library Cataloguing-in-Publication Data
A catalogue record for this book is available from the British Library.

Typeset by Fakenham Photosetting Limited, Fakenham, Norfolk
Printed and bound in Great Britain by Biddles Ltd
www.biddles.co.uk

Contents

Preface

'Gnosis' always seems to be topical. Yet hardly anyone
knows precisely what is meant by it, and many wise people
understand quite different things by it. Some radically
restrict the term to a small group of ancient Jews, Christians
and pagans, while others interpret 'gnosis' as a world
religion or secret 'undercurrent' throughout religious
history and the history of ideas; and yet others take the
term to denote a particular sort of philosophy of religion.
Recently a book on 'gnosis' even appeared, the purported
aim of which was 'to make a dubious term unusable': it
claimed to be 'Rethinking "Gnosticism"'.

In such a situation, big books should really have been
written on the many complexes of problems, taking up the
term 'gnosis' and what it denotes. I myself have written a
whole series of shorter articles and larger monographs on
individual problems associated with the term 'gnosis', but
here I am offering a short general survey before a detailed
overall account – in ancient terms the *epitome*, the abbreviated extract, before the *magnum opus*. A short survey is a
risky venture, in that it offers the interested reader only
theses and not a developed argument with all the evidence,
together with a critical discussion of the secondary
literature. At present we lack much of the necessary basis
for such an overall account: for example, so far there is no
consensus on dating the writings from the most extensive

find of ancient texts which can with good reason be assigned to a movement under the name of 'gnosis' (the library from Nag Hammadi in Upper Egypt, see below, 48–58). Whether many of these texts belong to the second, third or fourth centuries after Christ, and how precisely the complicated literary shaping of the existing material is to be described, is in dispute. In these circumstances a serious historian has to describe his account quite explicitly as an attempt and cannot conceal the degree to which such an outline is hypothetical.

This book arose out of a suggestion by Ulrich Nolte, which I gladly took up. I want to thank not only him, as my committed editor, but also two academic teachers who encouraged me to form my own picture of the history of ideas in antiquity, Luise Abramowski and Martin Hengel, of Tübingen. For the translations of the Nag Hammadi library I was able to refer to the first complete scholarly translation into German which the 'Berlin Study Group for Coptic-Gnostic Writings' have begun to publish this year (for the English translation of this book, the revised edition of the translation of the Nag Hammadi Library edited by James M. Robinson has been used). I am grateful to colleagues working with Hans-Gebhard Bethge and Hans-Martin Schenke for always giving me a warm welcome and for providing stimulating debates. I am again deeply grateful to John Bowden for presenting a German text in such a natural English version. Now I can only hope that even those whose picture of 'gnosis' does not correspond to my view will at least be prompted by what follows to re-examine some of the favourite certainties of the previous century. I hope that this short book will also help others to find reasonably reliable guidance on an unclear term and an obscure phenomenon.

Diverging from previous practice, I have decided as far as possible to translate Greek and Semitic terms like 'gnosis', 'gnostic' and 'Barbelo' into English. The very first Christian opponents of what in modern European scholarly research is subsumed under the everyday Greek word 'knowledge' ('gnosis') sought to emphasize the strangeness of the movement and the absurdities of its theories, and to this end as a rule did not translate expressions in a foreign language. That was already the case when the original Greek texts were translated into Latin, and usually it has remained the case to the present day. It has not helped an unprejudiced observation of the phenomena.

Christoph Markschies
Heidelberg, Summer 2002

I

Introduction

Given the difficulties posed by the term 'gnosis' which I
have already indicated, anyone who writes a short book on
the subject first of all has to give the reader some guidance
about what he thinks that the term really refers to. For
there is no usage of this term on which there is a consensus
in every respect and which is accepted everywhere. Nor,
things being as they are, can there be, since any definition
remains somewhat arbitrary.

1. The term 'gnosis'

The word 'gnosis' derives from the Greek and means
'knowledge'. It was used predominantly in philosophical
and religious contexts and did not denote 'knowing' a
person as a particular individual. Of course there are
exceptions: particular forms of the tradition of the
Hellenistic Alexander Romance use the word to describe
someone realizing that a particular person is Alexander the
Great (Version A, III 22, 15).

Sure knowledge, as distinct from mere perception, was
extremely important for Greek culture, which was
strongly orientated on rationality. The central position of
knowledge can be recognized in the philosophy of the
Athenian philosopher Plato (428/427–348/347 BC) and

takes the form of a strict philosophical system; according to
the philosopher's definition, the real being of things is
appropriated in knowledge. So there can be knowledge in
the primary sense only of the structures of all reality which
underlie the world of appearances, structures which Plato
calls 'ideas'. Right knowledge is the presupposition for
right action. Plato is convinced that such knowledge is
recollection, the restoration of a view that a person
originally had. The original knowledge has been lost and is
partially restored in a successful life through the understanding of what is seen. In Plato's school this apparently
highly abstract notion is translated into a concrete
philosophical training programme. In the context of a
community in which people live and learn together there
are exercises in 'turning the soul round', i.e. recognizing
individual things that can be perceived as representations
of elementary structures, which can be expressed as mathematical formulae. Thus in the end even the constitutive
principle of the structures is itself described mathematically
as the relationship between the original unity and the
subordinate multiplicity. In principle all human beings
have the capacity to see through the world perceived by the
senses in such a way: those who penetrate to a deeper
knowledge of the structures of reality are as like God as it is
possible for human beings to be (Plato, *Republic* 613c).

Of course such a significance of 'gnosis' is not limited to
Platonic philosophy. Aristotle described as the ideal of
successful life a life of 'theoretical contemplation', in other
words a life of reflection, without manual work, a '*bios
theoretikos*' wholly devoted to knowledge. Thus gnosis
becomes the goal of the whole of life, in the political sphere
as well as in religion and piety. Philosophy is a methodically
ordered form for attaining such 'gnosis'. According
to the Aristotelian philosophical teacher Alexander of
Aphrodisias (*c.* AD 200), too, 'Philosophy promises knowledge of being' (*Commentary on the Metaphysics of Aristotle* I,
307, 27).

This general striving for knowledge does not have any
specifically religious character, especially as it leads to very

varied results; the results among Aristotelians differ from those among Epicureans, Stoics or Platonists. For example, the Epicureans saw the imitation of the blissful life of the gods, who in their view had no direct influence on the nature of this world, as 'knowledge of the gods'. From the Hellenistic period onwards, the notion begins to spread in Greece that knowledge is not only the consequence of a committed activity of the human mind, or, more precisely, of the reason which indwells the world, the Logos, but a gift of grace by a God who would remain unknowable without this gift. It is already clear for the philosophy of Plato that the strict modern demarcations between philosophy and religion or theology do not hold at this point: someone who calls regaining original knowledge 'becoming like God' and seeks to attain it in a life in community with others of a like mind does not make a distinction between a philosophy with a neutral world-view and a theology with a religious orientation. Since 'like is always known by like', the predicate 'divine' links the one who knows to what he knows and to the one who gives knowledge. From the Hellenistic period onwards the religious connotations of the term 'gnosis' became more marked. Thus around AD 110 the writer Plutarch from Boeotia derived the name *Iseion*, Isis sanctuary, from 'coming to know being', and remarked: 'The name of the sanctuary promises knowledge of being. It is called Iseion to show that we will come to know being if in a rational and holy disposition we enter the sanctuary of the god' (*De Iside et Osiride* 2, 352A).

There is also a comparably high valuation of 'gnosis', 'knowledge', in the Jewish tradition, especially in the writings of Greek-speaking Jews. Above all the Greek translation of the so-called Jewish 'wisdom writings', some of which in the later period of antiquity came to be included in the canon of the Bible of Judaism and then also of the Christian 'Old Testament', is stamped by a corresponding terminology: 'The Lord gives wisdom; from his mouth come knowledge and understanding' (Prov. 2.60, and so the truly righteous man can boast that he 'has knowledge of God' (Wisd. 2.13). But this 'gnosis' has considerable importance for the life of the pious: 'To know you is perfect righteousness, and to know your power is the root of immortality' (Wisd. 15.3). This verse seeks to make it clear that the knowledge of God allows right political action and is even a help beyond death. We get a comparable impression of the significance of 'knowledge' if we look for the Hebrew and Aramaic equivalents of the Greek term 'gnosis' in the writings of the Qumran community by the Dead Sea; while this represents a particular tendency of intertestamental Judaism, it is just as much concerned with religious knowledge as other currents of contemporary Judaism.

Both pagan and Jewish antiquity valued 'knowledge', but their particular concepts of 'gnosis' had élitist features. Knowledge was not open to everyone. The most varied tendencies and forms of cult in antiquity were agreed on this fact. However, this élite which was capable of knowledge was defined in very different ways, and these differences are important in a comparison. Platonism identified the élite of those who had the highest form of knowledge (namely knowledge of the divine which could be expressed in mathematical formulae) with the group of philosophers, or more precisely with that group of philosophers which philosophized in a Platonic way. A strict distinction was made between a public and a non-public dimension of philosophy; certain higher elements of philosophy were intended only for oral communication, and these might be heard only by specially selected pupils. In the ancient religious form of the so-called mystery cults, like the mysteries of Isis or Mithras, which were popular above all at the time of the Roman empire, those who were initiated into the cult and therefore knew the secret cultic formulae formed the élite, and thus had that secret knowledge which made it easy for them to cope with death and the transition to immortality. However, the term 'knowledge' does not seem to have played a specific role.

In Hellenistic Judaism it was above all the group of god-fearing wise men, those who strove for knowledge and observed God's commandments, that formed an élite.

From the beginning, the Christianity that was taking shape also knew an élite of those with knowledge. However, we must ask whether this is really comparable with the other conceptions of an élite mentioned above. Thus according to a narrative in the Gospel of Mark, those who heard the teaching of Jesus in the synagogue of Nazareth marvelled that here a carpenter – not a member of the élite of educated scribes who were traditionally associated with 'knowledge' – was giving teaching about wisdom (Mark 6.1–3). Of course Christians, too, like Jews and pagans, also strove for 'gnosis'; they were interested in what philosophers were seeking and what other religious groups promised. The letter of Paul to the Christian community in Corinth, which has been handed down in the New Testament, documents for the middle of the first century the fact that the members of the Christian community in the port were proud of certain higher insights into revelation. The apostle writes that these Christians 'have become rich ... in all knowledge' (1 Cor. 4). So it could be said that in this form of Christianity a particular group formed an élite on the basis of its 'knowledge'. But Paul's criticism is that 'knowledge puffs up' (1 Cor. 8.1) and he rejected the wisdom of the Corinthians, which was orientated on earthly criteria. For his own conception, which distinguished between Christians who had come of age and those who had not, quite a different orientation was necessary: he preached a crucified man as saviour of the world, 'to the Jews a stumbling-block and to the Greeks folly' (1 Cor. 1.23), and saw the criterion of true knowledge here. At the end of the first and beginning of the second century the unknown author of the New Testament 'Letter to Timothy', which was published under the pseudonym of the apostle Paul and which stands in the tradition of his school, engages in polemic against 'the godless chatter and contradictions of what is falsely called knowledge' (1 Tim. 6.20f.). As the polemic continues, it becomes clear that certain people within the Christian community claimed 'knowledge', 'gnosis', for themselves and thus in the author's view 'miss the mark as regards the faith'.

Unfortunately we do not learn more, so this obscure passage has become a magnet for a long line of attempts at interpretation. Even in antiquity, within the framework of commentary on the Bible, the 'knowledge', 'gnosis', claimed by the opponents of the unknown author was connected with the expression *gnostikoi*, 'gnostics', or literally 'knowers' (Cramer VII, 51), and thus with the movement that is called 'gnosis'. So even now there is a tendency to assume that here we have a first piece of evidence for a religious movement designating itself as 'gnosis', 'knowledge'. But the passage only says that people within the Christian community were claiming for themselves what pagan philosophers and Jewish wisdom teachers were communicating, namely 'knowledge', and that their claim was disputed by the author of a writing which was later included in the New Testament of the Christian Bible. Another passage in the letter contains polemic against 'myths and endless genealogies' (1 Tim. 1.4), which gives us at least rather more of an idea of the 'knowledge' of the group under attack. These were presumably mythological expansions, above all of the biblical stories of the creation of the world, and in addition of the genealogies reported in the first book of the Bible, which were also developed and retold by other groups in Judaism at the time of the Roman empire. However, at the beginning of the second century a far simpler form of Christian theorizing could be put under the same heading of 'knowledge': a theological dissertation from this time in the form of a letter, the so-called 'Letter of Barnabas', was written so that its readers would have 'perfect knowledge' (*gnosis*) in addition to their faith (Letter of Barnabas 1, 5). Now according to the author's view, 'perfect knowledge' merely means expounding the Bible of the Jews, the book that was later called the 'Old Testament', in the light of the person of Jesus Christ, and conversely expounding the person of Jesus Christ in the light of the Bible. At another point the unknown author says that the 'knowledge' given to the Christians helps them to take the way of life and to avoid the darkness (19,1). Thus there was no unitary concept of 'knowledge' among Christians as early as the beginning of the second century.

The picture that we get of the importance of the key word 'knowledge' in early Christianity changes only for the last third of the second century. At the same time it becomes clearer. The Middle-Platonic philosopher Celsus from Alexandria attests in polemic against the Christians from this period that among them there are people 'who claim to be knowers', and his later Christian opponent expands the quotation, 'just as the Epicureans call themselves "philosophers"' (Origen, *Against Celsus* V, 61). Evidently at this time there were quite specific people who called themselves 'knowing' in the sense of the modern term 'intellectuals' and had a 'knowledge' to offer. But here too, it is not said either that a separate religion existed which called itself 'knowledge' or that a whole group of intellectual tendencies would use the term in question to describe themselves. Rather, the key term 'knowers' is the designation applied to itself by a quite specific group within early Christianity, which made it clear that it wanted to hand on in a superlative way the 'knowledge' that almost all contemporary offers of meaning claimed to have.

The Greek word which occurs here – *gnostikoi*, 'knowers' – is usually rendered 'gnostic' in English and not translated, although it is a word from philosophical technical terminology. We owe the term itself to Plato, who coined several hundred Greek terms with the ending *-ikos*. *Gnostikē epistēmē*, 'understanding connected with knowledge', denotes mathematical sciences as opposed to *praktikē epistēmē*, 'understanding connected with practice' (*Politics* 258E). The word was rarely used by philosophers and remained limited above all to the Platonic tradition: for example, Platonists call the cognitive element of the divine soul '*to gnostikon*', the capacity to know. So the term did not refer to a person as a whole but to particular capacities of a person.

Of course even the self-designation 'knowers' for members of a group within the Christian community, which is also attested in Celsus and Origen, does not represent any precise criterion for demarcation from other tendencies. Members of the most varied intellectual tendencies and forms of religion in antiquity wanted to be 'knowers', even if they did not give themselves this name, or precisely because they did not do so. Therefore the claim to knowledge made by the Christian groups of 'knowers' in question could also be disputed: a Christian theologian from Alexandria by the name of Titus Flavius Clemens (Clement), who is strongly influenced by contemporary Platonism and likewise writes at the end of the second and beginning of the third century, documents this. He stands wholly in the Platonic tradition, and for him 'knowledge', 'gnosis', is also the true goal of Christian life and thought. 'Gnosis' is a description of Christian faith, and as a 'true gnostic' the church Christian can be opposed to the adherents of a gnosis which is wrongly so-called: 'And I am also surprised that some dare to call themselves perfect and knowing (gnostic), puffing themselves up and elevating themselves ... above the apostle (Paul)' (*Tutor*, I, 52, 2). According to Clement, the false 'knowers' do not understand that strict philosophical criteria apply to correct knowledge and true knowing, and so their intellectual weakness becomes evident in an ethic for which Clement has nothing but contempt: 'I recall encountering a sect, the leader of which claimed that he fought pleasure with pleasure. This worthy knower (gnostic) – in fact he really said that he was also a knower – advanced on pleasure in feigned combat' (*Carpets* II, 117, 5). Clement also accuses 'the adherents of Prodicus' of such ethical libertinism: 'misusing the name, they call themselves knowers (gnostics) and claim that by nature they are sons of the first God; but they misuse ... their freedom and live as they want' (*Carpets* III, 30, 1). By contrast, according to Clement the 'perfect knower' is a philosopher who is constantly occupied, first with the theoretical contemplation of things in the framework of a Christianized Platonic picture of the world; secondly with fulfilling the commandments laid down in the two testaments of the Bible; and – likewise continuing the communal life and learning of the Platonic tradition – thirdly with the training of competent men: 'The combination of all three makes the perfect knower' (*Carpets* II, 46, 1).

Because members of particular groups of Christians designated themselves 'knowers' in this way and thus made clear their special claim to 'knowledge', from the end of the second century Christian theologians could sum up the concern of further groups with a similar make-up under the term 'knowledge' in ever cruder caricatures. A pioneer in this indiscriminating extension of the designation in the interests of polemic was a Greek theologian named Irenaeus, who lived in Lyons. Around AD 180 he composed a five-volume work under the title 'Disproof and Refutation of Knowledge Wrongly So-Called', and in so doing summed up the concern of a large number of groups and persons under the one keyword 'knowledge'. However, interestingly he did not apply the term 'knowers', i.e. 'gnostics', to all representatives of 'gnosis', 'knowledge', but differentiated between them by heads of schools, a practice customary in his time in designating philosophical schools. Only of one particular group does Irenaeus say: 'And they call themselves "gnostics"' (*Refutation* I, 25, 6; cf. I, 11, 1). Unfortunately we do not know how this group relates to the groups of knowers mentioned in Celsus and Clement. But it is not very probable that they are identical, so that we can assume that at the end of the second century a variety of groups of Christians called themselves 'knowers'. It is no longer possible to shed more light on why they gave themselves this name, since, as I have remarked, to have 'knowledge' is not a specific characteristic, but 'absolute banality' (cf. Bentley Layton, 'Prolegomena', 339).

Alongside the 'knowers' Irenaeus describes the whole series of further groups; with polemical undertones he attributes 'knowledge' to them, but their members evidently did not describe themselves as 'knowers'. Whereas since the eighteenth century scholars have not only included them within 'gnosis' but have also termed their members 'gnostics', by contrast Irenaeus still reports conflict between them and the 'gnostics' (II, 13, 9).

Furthermore, just how problematical it is to follow the
tradition of modern European scholarship in bringing
together a wealth of ancient groups under the one keyword
'knowledge' and calling their members 'gnostics' is evident
from a look at the mass of self-designations which have
been handed down in the texts usually assigned to 'gnosis'.
'They call themselves Christians,' wrote the theologian
Justin in Rome in the middle of the second century with
admirable openness, thus indirectly conceding that the
designations of groups of 'gnosis' by heads of schools
('Marcians, Valentinians, Basilidians, or Satornilians')
which is still customary today were names given by critics of
the whole trend (*Dialogue with Trypho* 35, 6).

Other self-designations were more specific, and give first
indications of a self-understanding: for example, one group
calls itself 'the perfect', 'since in their view no one
approaches the greatness of their knowledge' (Irenaeus,
Refutation I, 13, 6). The relevant term 'knowers', '*gnostikoi*',
does not occur in the great library discovered at Nag
Hammadi, but there is evidence of a large number of such
self-designations, some of which do not seem very specific,
and some of which already refer to particular points of the
teaching of this individual group: 'Sons of God' (EpJac,
NHC I, 2, 11, 1, etc.); 'the elect' (TractTrip, NHC, I, 5, 135,
5, etc.) or 'the solitary' (EvThom, NHC II, 2, sayings 16,
49), and also 'the descendants of Seth' (EvEg, NHC III, 2,
56, 3 and 17, etc.); 'children of the bridal chamber'
(EvPhil, NHC II, 3, saying 87 [72, 21f.]) and 'the fourth,
kingless and perfect race' (OW, NHC II, 5, 125, 6). With
the name 'Seth', borne in the Bible by Adam's son (Gen.
4.25), an image of God (Gen. 5.3), a writer put himself in
the tradition of a figure to whom, according to ancient
Jewish views, Adam had entrusted special heavenly
mysteries (Life of Adam and Eve 25–9), and who in
rabbinic Judaism can also symbolize the 'king Messiah'
(Midrash Bereshith Rabba on Genesis 4.26). 'Children of
the bridal chamber' alludes to a 'sacrament of the bridal
chamber' which will be discussed later (p. 114.). The last-
mentioned self-designation, 'the fourth, kingless and

perfect race', surpasses the self-designation 'the third race', which was widespread among Christians: just as the normal church Christians felt superior as the third race to the two other races, the Jews and the Gentiles, so these perfect Christians felt superior to ordinary Christians.

To sum up, then, we must maintain that to bring together a great variety of ancient groups or even intellectual currents under the terms 'gnosis' and 'gnosticism' in modern Europe is to follow a strategy adopted by Christian theologians in antiquity, who sum up under the everyday word 'knowledge' diverse movements to which knowledge was as important as it was to many other intellectual currents and forms of religion of the time. Here the self-designation 'knower', which in antiquity was used by quite specific groups of Christians, was extended to all members of a movement going by the name of 'knowledge', the existence of which, following certain theologians of antiquity, was presupposed unquestioningly.

Since the eighteenth century the term 'gnosis' has increasingly moved away from its origins. It has been used more and more markedly as an interpretative category for contemporary philosophical and religious movements; a few examples can demonstrate this. In 1835 a book by the Tübingen New Testament scholar Ferdinand Christian Baur (1792–1860) was published under the title *Die christliche Gnosis oder die christliche Religions-Philosophie in ihrer geschichtlichen Entwicklung* ('Christian Gnosis or the Historical Development of the Christian Philosophy of Religion'), in which 'gnosis' was understood against the background of an idealistic approach as a form of mediation between God and the world transcending time, which, it was claimed, was the constant element in all philosophy of religion. Baur reconstructed a development of 'gnosis' which culminated in the Berlin philosopher Hegel's philosophy of religion: elements of the three religions, Judaism, Christianity and paganism – like the Jewish notion of a creator of the world, the Christian notion of the figure of Christ and the pagan notion of matter – were organically combined into a philosophy of religion and communicated by principles like that of 'evolution', development (*Die christliche Gnosis*, 25–9). Thus 'gnosis' presupposed an awareness of both the unity and the diversity of religions (ibid., 67); the various doctrinal systems could be classified by their relationship to the three religions (ibid., 108). Consequently Baur saw between gnosticism and Christianity 'a contradiction extending to the great and general, an intellectual attitude which diverges in the whole' (*Das manichäische Religionssystem*, 1831, 1). On the other hand he claimed an 'ongoing identity and continuity of the direction once taken' between ancient 'gnosis' and the 'more recent philosophy of religion' of a Schelling or Hegel (*Die christliche Gnosis*, 736). The Berlin philosopher Johann Gottlieb Fichte (1762–1814) also designated part of the Protestant theology of his time 'gnosticism' (*Grundzüge des gegenwärtigen Zeitalters*, Werke VII, 1845, 101–3). However, by that he understood a 'system in Christianity' which followed the maxim 'that the concept is judge' (101). Fichte dismissed this position on the grounds that the Bible or the oral tradition had this function of judge in the dispute between theologians. Whereas the great theologians at the time of the Reformation had still insisted that the Bible was the sole criterion and pointed out to their opponents the connection between scripture and tradition, in the bosom of Protestantism 'a new gnosticism soon came into being ... establishing the principle that the Bible had to be explained rationally'. Fichte's polemic was directed against the Protestant theology of the eighteenth century: 'This was said to be as rational as these gnostics were themselves: but they were as rational as the worst philosophical system of all' (103). The extreme extension of the sphere which for two centuries has been designated 'gnosis' becomes particularly clear if we look at the theosophical movement and anthroposophy. Parts of this movement spoke of themselves as a 'gnostic church'. Rudolf Steiner (1861–1925) used the term 'gnosis' to denote a higher mode of knowledge standing above philosophy, and was therefore seen by some as the very model of a 'modern gnostic'. Above all most recently, people have been fond of talking about a 'revival of gnosis' to characterize diverse movements connected with esotericism and the New Age. Such extensions of the use of the term do not help towards a precise understanding of what early Christian theologians designated 'gnosis'.

2. 'Gnosis' or 'gnosticism'?

As the ancient term 'gnosis' is only of very limited use for focusing precisely on the phenomenon of the history of ideas and the history of religion which since antiquity has been labelled 'knowledge', time and again attempts have been made to determine or even define the phenomenon in another way. The most influential definition was attempted in the twentieth century at one of the first great scholarly conferences to devote itself to the topic.

In order to end the terminological confusion associated with the term 'gnosis' since the nineteenth century, more than 30 years ago a proposal was developed which for a time shaped the discussion but could not win through and was controversial from the very beginning. On 18 April 1966, the last day of the great Gnosis Congress in Messina, the participants approved a concluding document cautiously entitled 'Proposal', which was prefaced to the proceedings in various European languages. It had been prepared by an international commission made up of experts in religious studies, theologians and philosophers of religion. In this concluding document of Messina the proposal was 'by the simultaneous application of historical and typological methods' to designate 'a particular group of systems of the second century after Christ' as 'gnosticism', and to use 'gnosis' to define a conception of knowledge transcending the times which was described as 'knowledge of divine mysteries for an élite'. So the conference distinguished those ancient movements which were called 'knowledge', 'gnosis', by their opponents, from 'gnosis' proper by using a new designation ('gnosticism').

An attempt was made in Messina to reduce conceptual confusion, but this caused new uncertainty, because something was being called 'gnosticism' that the ancient theologians had called 'gnosis'.

Moreover the term 'gnosticism', which the Messina conference proposed should be applied to the ancient movement, is not an ancient word. The 'knowers' did not in fact call themselves 'gnosticists' but 'gnostics'. The expression is quite modern in origin and derives from the English philosopher and theologian Henry More (1614–87), who was fellow of Christ's College, Cambridge, and one of the 'Cambridge Platonists', the advocates of a philosophical theology stamped by Platonism and Neoplatonism. However, the terminological proposal of Messina was diametrically opposed to the way in which the English philosopher used the term 'gnosticism': Henry More was following an earlier English tradition in summing up under the name 'gnosticks' not only the adherents of quite specific groups assigned to 'knowledge' in antiquity but all Christian heresies. Diverging from previous practice, More now designated these as 'gnosticisme', and thus gave the name 'gnosticism' to that particular form which was superior to 'gnosis' in the real sense, whereas the conference in Messina in 1966 proposed the opposite course – evidently in ignorance of the history of the term. Whereas for More 'gnosticism' denoted the primal Christian heresy, which stems from intellectual over-confidence and ethical forgetfulness of the self, those who took part in the Messina conference around 300 years later had a more positive understanding of their overarching concept, now called 'gnosis', as 'a knowledge of divine mysteries reserved for an élite'. Here the Messina concept of 'gnosis' no longer stands in a specific relationship to Christianity, at any rate in a relationship comparable to More's definition of 'gnosis' as a 'primal Christian heresy', but describes a general attitude of mind and form of existence. But what precisely has to be imagined by this is left quite unclear in the Messina document. The proposal of the conference on the essence and characteristics of 'gnosis' does not say very much more than the formula quoted above about 'knowledge of divine mysteries reserved for an élite'. According to the Messina proposal, is classical Platonism 'gnosis'? In a sense it is, since here knowledge of the divine mysteries is reserved for an élite. Are Freemasons 'gnostics'? In a sense they are, since they reserve the knowledge of the divine mysteries for an élite.

So on the one hand by separating the term 'gnosis' from 'gnosticism' and on the other hand by its relatively brief characterization of 'gnosis', the Messina proposal led to quite a wide and general concept of gnosis which is almost unusable for the historian. For we saw that in antiquity almost everyone was agreed that 'knowledge', 'gnosis', was particularly valuable, but on the other hand there was a vigorous dispute about the form of true knowledge and how it was to be distinguished from pseudo-knowledge. There was as yet no unitary conception of 'knowledge' in antiquity. This fact was evidently not noted in Messina. On the other hand, in view of the subsequent meteoric career of the term 'gnosis' at the end of the twentieth century, we have to say that in attempting a terminological shift the conference was in fact merely describing the actual use of the term in the years after the Second World War and drawing conclusions from it.

Since, as the previous paragraphs have shown, to bring together specific ancient groups and intellectual currents into a movement under the name of 'gnosis' and to designate their representatives 'gnostics' represents a modern development of an ancient Christian polemic, 'gnosis' in the strict sense remains what Michael Allen Williams has called a 'typological construct' of modern scholarship. However, in historical study it can make sense to work with such typological constructs if they also help to see phenomena with related content. In the end it is not only hard to dispute that some of the ancient movements usually brought together under the heading 'gnosis' are actually very closely connected both in content and in outward form, but also necessary to recognize that some of their influence extends to the present. In an account we need only distinguish carefully between those phenomena which are associated through direct historical connections, those which are connected more indirectly through a common cultural climate, and those between which a typological connection can be made through agreements in content.

In the next section I shall present a model which is the basis for the present book and which builds on a certain consensus in research into gnosis. In this way, of course, I am initially postulating no more than how various phenomena belong together in terms of content; only in the course of the discussion will it be possible to demonstrate whether the phenomena themselves in fact belong together. Here I shall use the term 'typological', which is comparatively rare in German scholarly theory, to bring out the continuity with the discussion which led to the attempt at a definition in Messina.

3. 'Gnosis' – a typological model

In what follows, by 'gnosis' I understand those movements which express their particular interest in the rational comprehension of the state of things by insight ('knowledge') in theological systems that as a rule are characterized by a particular collection of ideas or motives in the texts.

1. The experience of a completely other-worldly, distant, supreme God;

2. the introduction, which among other things is conditioned by this, of further divine figures, or the splitting up of existing figures into figures that are closer to human beings than the remote supreme God';

3. the estimation of the world and matter as evil creation and an experience, conditioned by this, of the alienation of the gnostic in the world;

4. the introduction of a distinct creator God or

assistant: within the Platonic tradition he is called 'craftsman' – Greek *demiurgos* – and is sometimes described as merely ignorant, but sometimes also as evil;

5. the explanation of this state of affairs by a mytho-logical drama in which a divine element that falls from its sphere into an evil world slumbers in human beings of one class as a divine spark and can be freed from this;

6. knowledge ('gnosis') about this state, which, however, can be gained only through a redeemer figure from the other world who descends from a higher sphere and ascends to it again;

7. the redemption of human beings through the knowledge of 'that God (or the spark) in them' (TestVer, NHC IX, 3, 56, 15–20), and finally

8. a tendency towards dualism in different types which can express itself in the concept of God, in the opposition of spirit and manner, and in anthropology.

This typological model, which is used as a basis here, corre-sponds, moreover, to the concept of 'gnosis' depicted by many ancient Christian theologians and non-Christian thinkers.

Before we reconstruct a history of the development of 'gnostic' movements in antiquity using this model, it is necessary also to take a brief look at the main problems of recent research into gnosis. Here it will become clear what factors in addition to those already mentioned shape the various pictures of the phenomenon of 'gnosis'.

4. The main problems in recent discussion

Even before the application of a constructivist hermeneutic to the problem in the 1990s, there was a wide-ranging consensus that talk of 'gnosis' in antiquity and in the present to a large degree represents a modern typological construction. It was also agreed that the typological construction leaves a very marked stamp on the mass of historical phenomena covered by such a model.

These connections can be made clear by means of a prominent example which at the same time brings out the close connection between the course of more recent research into gnosis and the general history of ideas and culture. In his epoch-making work *Gnosis und Spätantiker Geist* ('Gnosis and the Spirit of Late Antiquity'), which began to appear in 1934 and then initially was discontinued because of the author's emigration, the Jewish philosopher Hans Jonas (1903–93) initially attempted to work out the basic character of gnosis with the aid of an existentialist analysis indebted to Martin Heidegger. Like Ferdinand Christian Baur around a century previously (see above, p. 11), Jonas set out to describe the historical evidence in terms of its internal composition and not to put it in purely chronological order. He included in 'gnosis' both the Jewish-Hellenistic theologian Philo of Alexandria, a contemporary of Paul, and Plotinus, the founder of Neoplatonism in the third century AD, because he saw them both as being likewise stamped by the existential starting point which also governed those Christian thinkers who are traditionally reckoned to be in the movement: 'an oppressed existence made itself known there, anxious about its riddle and concerned to find an answer' (Jonas, *Wissenschaft als persönliches Erlebnis*, 1987, 17). Jonas described the basic make-up of gnosis as being the experience of solitude, of being exposed in an inhospitable foreign land. The true homeland of human beings lay in an other-worldly realm of light, while the world was experienced as a realm of darkness remote from God. For Jonas, the most distinctive gnostic attitude to existence therefore consists in a revolutionary anti-cosmic orientation of life and thought which he regards as so characteristic of the time of the Roman empire that he sees the 'spirit of late antiquity' defined by a 'gnostic age'. In this way research into gnosticism may have been freed from the ghetto of the specialists, but at the price of a very radical extension of the phenomena relevant to an account under the heading of 'gnosis'. Later Jonas also compared the extreme separation of human beings and the world in 'gnosis' with 'modern existentialism and its nihilistic aspects' (*Gnosis* II, 363), in essence making structurally impossible a really strict chronological demarcation of the phenomenon by the perspective chosen. These problems seem to have become clear to Jonas himself: more than 30 years later, at the 1966 Messina Conference, which has already been mentioned, he departed from his first scheme in attempting a typological and historical demarcation of the phenomenon of 'gnosis' in which, for example, there was no explicit mention of the Neoplatonic philosopher Plotinus, so that one could assume that he had made his typological model more precise and in this way reduced the mass of historical phenomena to which he applied it.

However, the extremely diverse picture of 'gnosis' in many more recent accounts stems not only from the fact that in such a construction, in other words in the definition of a phenomenon by means of a catalogue of motifs, the scope can become either narrower or wider, but also from a series of further factors and prior judgements. These have an effect on the extent of such a catalogue of gnostic motifs and thus on the typological model, but they are not determined in a strict sense by the model.

The most important prior judgement is whether one merely wants to assign the phenomenon of 'gnosis' to a religion or regards it as a movement which goes beyond the limits of a single religion.

In the first instance 'gnosis' is understood as a movement within the Christian religion, and occasionally also interpreted as a form of the philosophy of religion which already had its foundation in, or came into being in, Judaism. This understanding already emerged in antiquity, was applied by Christian theologians, but likewise was championed by pagan philosophers. That did not and does not of course exclude the fact that a wealth of stimuli from other religions and philosophical contexts influenced 'gnosis'. This suggests an interpretation of gnosis as a

particular philosophical interpretation of Christianity of
the kind put forward by ancient theologians like
Hippolytus of Rome (beginning of the third century), and
also the German church historian and scientific organizer
Adolf von Harnack (1851–1930). The interpretation
resulted in, and still results in, the value judgement that
the whole of 'gnosis' is the result of a failed attempt at
a 'higher' interpretation of the theologoumena of
the majority church, which was therefore rejected by the
majority church.

In the second instance 'gnosis' is understood as a world-
view or religion which can adapt to various religions but
nevertheless always remains different from them. The gist
of this interpretation was prepared for by the extension of
the range of subject-matter to which the term was applied
from the eighteenth century onwards, and basically
followed systematically from the 'gnosis' interpretations of
German idealistic philosophy and existentialist ontology
in the nineteenth and twentieth centuries. It became
dominant from the middle of the twentieth century
onwards. This interpretation was formulated programmati-
cally by the Dutch scholar Gilles Quispel (born 1916) with
the title of his book *Gnosis als Weltreligion* ('Gnosis as a
World Religion') (1951). The metaphor chosen to describe
this perspective is not unproblematical, because it is really
rather unfriendly: 'gnosis' is said to nest in a parasitical way
in a 'host religion' and is compared – usually uninten-
tionally – with a pest. The kind of Christian gnosis
constitutive of the other picture would then ultimately
be a contradiction in terms, as Karl Wolfgang Tröger
pointed out.

Thus the directions of both interpretations differ in
their view of the relations between 'gnosis' and
Christianity. In the first instance 'gnosis' is possibly
originally a pre-Christian movement, but at all events over
long stretches is shaped by people who claimed to be
Christians. The judgement as to whether this claim is
appropriate has therefore for some time now been made
more cautiously than in antiquity and early modernity,

because it is becoming increasingly clear that Christianity took shape only in the second and third centuries and defined its limits by both linking up with its environment and opposing it. In the other instance, gnosis is a priori a movement outside Christianity and a non-Christian movement which for a time assimilated to Christianity. Each of these two interpretations is connected with a thesis about the historical development of 'gnosis': anyone who assumes that the movement originally came into being in Judaism and Christianity will either attribute to a pre-Christian Jewish gnosis those non-Christian texts which occur in the ancient material and on the basis of a typological affinity can be assigned to 'gnosis', or regard them as texts the authors of which covered up or deleted the reference to an original spiritual home in the course of an increasing demonization of 'gnosis' within Christianity. By contrast, those who regard 'gnosis' a priori as a non-Christian movement or a movement outside Christianity will regard non-Christian gnostic texts as admirable evidence for their point of view. There is also considerable dispute as to whether 'gnosis' in essence represents a religion – in other words is an independent attempt in the face of the experience of contingency to depict with the help of myth and cult a category of meaning which transcends this world – or rather an attempt to understand the Jewish-Christian religion better, orientated on the philosophical standards of antiquity. Whereas in the first model texts orientated on philosophical standards are the really characteristic texts of the movement, for the second model they are merely a form in which the 'gnostics' speak about their religion. Of course at this point much depends on how one reconstructs standards of philosophical argumentation (and communal living) in antiquity.

Thus above all the beginnings are a matter of dispute in more recent research into gnosis. The situation looks different from the end of antiquity: both interpretative approaches agree that at any rate ancient gnosis culminated and in a certain sense also ended in the foundation of a separate religion, Manichaeism, named after the

Persian thinker Mani. Ferdinand Christian Baur already
saw this in his 1831 account of the Manichaean system of
religion, *Das manichäische Religionssystem*, which interpreted
Manichaeism as 'an implementation of the gnostic
principle carried through with great consistency' and
explained 'an even sharper opposition to Christianity' from
this (*Religionssystem*, 2). Mani (AD 216–77) attempted to
bring together three great world religions of antiquity,
Christianity, Zoroastrianism and Buddhism, and in this way
to offer a single common religion to the land in which he
lived, the Persian Sassanid empire. To this end he began
intensive missionary work among adherents of these three
religions. There can be no doubt at all that in the course of
the missionary preaching the Manichaean religious system
could be expressed more strongly against a Christian,
Zoroastrian or Buddhist background – the extant sources
show that clearly. Moreover, the most famous early Latin
theologian, the North African Augustine, could become a
Manichaean for a while in the firm conviction that he
could remain a Christian and was merely learning a
deeper understanding of Christianity (this was in the years
373–82). To this degree it is true at least for Manichaeism
that this 'gnostic system' adapted itself to existing forms of
religion – here representatives of the two interpretative
approaches could use the image of a parasitical form of
religion, were it not intrinsically problematical because
of the value judgement contained in it.

As well as the prior judgement already mentioned,
further factors were and are responsible for the various
pictures of 'gnosis'. Here I shall mention just the two most
important. First, there is the general history of the scholarly
disciplines which have taken part in investigating the
phenomenon; and secondly, there is a specific situation
which has been defined, and time and again changed, by a
number of striking textual discoveries.

The history of research into Manichaeism in particular
shows how closely the development of more recent
research is bound up with the history of the disciplines
involved in it. If we are to understand the amazingly rapid

dissemination of the image of gnosis as an independent world religion, we must be clear that from the late nineteenth century onwards an autonomous study of religion increasingly came to be established at the universities, independent of theology, and that there was great interest in recognizing the premises of particular pictures of the history of religion and isolating them from the phenomena. A formula from the last major comprehensive German account which draws a distinction between the 'narrowness of church history' and the 'free air of the history of religion' (Rudolph, *Gnosis*, 37) is significant for such perspectives.

Moreover, the history of research shows particularly clearly that the historical picture of 'gnosis' has changed markedly by contrast with the schemes of antiquity and early modernity, above all following the major discoveries of texts in the nineteenth and twentieth centuries. But here research was dependent on the one hand on the particular state of philological and editorial efforts and on the other hand on the competence of an individual scholar who had been occupied with this field: knowledge of Greek, Latin, Syriac, Coptic, Arabic, Turkish (Ugrian) and Chinese texts, along with texts in four Persian dialects, is necessary for researching into Manichaeism; and by no means all the texts discovered in the twentieth century are available in critical editions. Here texts which were purchased in the 1930s and which presumably came from a library in Medinet Madi, a military colony in the south of the Fayum, are particularly remarkable. In recent years, important finds have also come to light in a desert oasis on the west of Egypt by the name of Dakleh, interestingly in an archaeological context which indicates 'gnostics'. The exploration of these finds is still in its infancy.

The discovery of texts at Nag Hammadi, which has already been mentioned, also required great philological efforts, because the tractates, originally written in Greek, were discovered in forms of Coptic dialect for which there were no reliable grammars or lexica at the time of the discovery. In this way much attention had to be paid to opening up the language of the text, and a remarkably refined philology of Persian and Coptic dialects came into being. Because of that, however, the investigation of the tradition history of the writing and their historical context took a back place: in other words, the initially great philological problems of the texts and the special situation of the discipline of the study of religion meant that 'gnosis' was more markedly perceived as an independent movement and religion then it would perhaps have been in other circumstances.

Whereas for the reasons mentioned the second model, that of understanding 'gnosis' as an independent, non-Christian religion, was the most far-reaching consensus among scholars, above all in the second half of the twentieth century, this unity has been shattered in recent years, and as in many other areas the present situation is characterized by a new diversity of models. The discovery that there is no single 'gnostic myth' but a variety of myths which cannot be derived from a single original myth was also essentially responsible for this – we can already find a similar observation in various Christian authors of antiquity. However, it is expressed in a polemical form, as when the various outlines of systems are compared with the Hydra, a mythological monster with nine heads which, as often as one head was cut off, grew two new ones (Irenaeus of Lyons, *Refutation* I, 30, 15; Hippolytus, *Refutation* V, 11). This at the same time led to the collapse of the central thesis of research, namely that a non-Christian myth was at the core of 'gnosis', the so-called myth of the 'redeemed redeemer'. Leading representatives of the 'history-of-religions school', a friendly alliance of the theologians and experts on religion at the beginning of the twentieth century, had postulated that 'gnosis' had taken over such a 'primordial man' myth in an altered form from the earliest sources of Zoroastrian, ancient Persian religion. Above all the New Testament scholar Wilhelm Bousset (1865–1920) and the history-of-religions expert Richard Reitzenstein (1861–1931), both for a time active in Göttingen, should be mentioned here. Bousset described the myth like this:

'There was an age-old myth which reported that the world came about through the sacrifice of the primal man, was formed from his body ... This myth then took a new turn to the degree that the Greek world of ideas consorted with oriental fantasies. The primal man sacrificed at the beginning of the creation of the world now becomes the *proanthropos* (Greek for the 'pre-man'), the firstborn of the supreme deity ... who at the beginning of the development of the world sinks down into matter or is seduced into matter and so provides the impetus for the creation of the world ... The primal man who descends into matter and is defeated here, and is liberated only laboriously and with the loss of his equipment of light, is clearly a cosmogonic potency. The whole development of the world is derived from the mixing of the parts of the light from the primal man with the elements of darkness' (Bousset, *Hauptprobleme der Gnosis*, 1907, 215–17). According to Reitzenstein, a mythical notion had already existed in Iran 'which regards the soul or the inner person as a divine being sent down into matter from the light world and again freed from it and recalled to it' (Reitzenstein, *Das iranische Erlösungsmysterium*, 1921, V). This 'primordial man' was the first to be redeemed and at the same time the redeemer for the rest of humankind, hence also the myth of the 'redeemed redeemer'.

The background to such constructions at the beginning of the twentieth century was enthusiasm about the discovery of new hitherto completely unknown ancient texts: on the expeditions of the Berlin Museum on the Silk Road and especially at the Chinese oasis of Turfan in the years between 1902 and 1914, a large number of larger or smaller fragments were collected containing texts in a great variety of oriental languages. At the time when Reitzenstein wrote about them, however, they had by no means been completely published. So the construct of a myth of the 'redeemed redeemer' and the derivation of ancient 'gnosis' from early Persian mythology that was built on it was on very shaky ground. Later, after the critical edition of the relevant passages, it proved, for example, that a central piece of Reitzenstein's evidence was not part of an ancient Zoroastrian text at all, but came from a cycle of Manichaean hymns. Because of this, among other things the derivation of a 'gnostic' myth of the 'primordial man' from the Zoroastrian religion had to be given up at the beginning of the 1960s. Two Berlin scholars, Carsten Colpe and Hans-Martin Schenke, dealt the death-blow to the old hypothesis of the 'history-of-religions school' with their dissertations of 1961 and 1962. On the other hand, there can be no doubt that a myth of the man which resembles the scheme once developed by Reitzenstein is attested in certain texts traditionally assigned to 'gnosis', though not in all. Relevant examples can be found above all in the texts found at Nag Hammadi: 'For this one, Adamas, is a light which radiated from the light; he is the eye of the light. For this is the first man, he through whom and to whom everything became ... He came down from above, for the annulment of the deficiency' (EvEg, NHC III, 2, 49, 8–16; cf. ibid., IV 2, 61, 8–18). Our example shows how complicated the situation has become after the collapse of the great hypotheses. Individual explanations must now be sought for a wealth of different texts from very different groups. That of course makes the question of the historical derivation and dissemination of individual ideas all the more urgent. Are they characteristically 'gnostic' at all? Or are they a combination of various Jewish and Christian speculations about biblical texts to which there is a clear allusion in our example (e.g. John 1.3: 'All things were made through him', or John 1.9, 'He [i.e. the incarnate word of God] was the true light')?

At the end of this brief section on the problems of more recent research into gnosis I return to an observation that I made in the section on the term 'gnosis'. The unity of a phenomenon named since antiquity with the Greek term of 'knowledge' is a comparatively loose one; it has existed for centuries above all on the basis of the typological constructions of scholars concerned to provide a clear ordering of things, whether for motives of 'combating heresy' or in the interest of a general history of ideas,

religion and culture. The more strongly this evidence is
perceived, the easier it is to explain the *de facto* plurality of
the approaches and use them creatively to understand
'gnosis'. In other words, the plurality of approaches in
recent years is appropriate in so far as it takes account of
the fact that the unitary phenomenon of 'gnosis' to which
all reconstructions relate exists only in the form of various
typological constructions. The historical chapters which
follow will, however, attempt to demonstrate that it makes
sense to consider particular phenomena by means of such
a model. At the end of the book we shall return once again
to the question of what effects what we have subsumed in
antiquity under the term 'gnosis' have had up to European
modernity and finally even up to the immediate present
(pp. 119–22).

II

———————

The Sources

A large number of written sources are available as the basis for a description of what Christian theologians in antiquity already subsumed under the heading of 'knowledge'. Here I shall describe them at length and set out their content at equal length, before describing the phenomenon of 'knowledge' itself and making an attempt to reconstruct its history. We saw that the phenomenon itself is a typological construct on the basis of specific sources. Therefore it is necessary first to form an independent judgement on this material. It can be put into four different groups.

First, there are texts some of which are quoted at great length by Christian authors who have a critical attitude to 'knowledge' and which they assign to the movement. Secondly, there are original texts which have survived separately, mostly in Coptic, and contain a large number of the eight motifs mentioned above. Furthermore, there are critical accounts and reports by the various ancient Christian 'heresy hunters' ('heresiologists'), though their value as sources must be examined critically against their particular overall tendency. And finally, there are those texts which in the light of our typological model must clearly be designated 'non-gnostic', but which contain individual motifs or combinations of motifs from the typological model cited above.

1. Ancient authors critical of 'gnosis', who hand on original texts

Irenaeus of Lyons

The first author to be mentioned in this group of sources is the bishop of the Greek-speaking community of Lyons at the end of the second century, Irenaeus, who came from Asia Minor. His main work, the five-volume *Conviction and Refutation of Knowledge Wrongly So-Called*, has survived complete only in a Latin translation from late antiquity and is usually cited with a not very specific Latin short title, *Adversus Haereses*, 'Against the Heresies'. The work was written presumably between AD 180 and 185 and was composed because the author wanted to react to problems in his diocese. The bishop had observed the activity of skilled Christian orators in his community in Gaul, which contained native Celts as well as Greek-speaking merchants, who 'with eloquence practised in deceit' – in other words, with some rhetorical skill – and considerable success argued for an intellectual 'quest' (*Refutation* I, Preface 1). If we take the title of his work into account, these people seem to have campaigned within the Christian community for a quest for 'knowledge'. Irenaeus accused them not only of disseminating false teaching which deviated from the essential core of Christianity but also of exploring their positions with merely superficial thinking: 'I want, in accordance with my modest competence, to indicate starting points for their refutation by showing that what they say is absurd and confused and cannot be reconciled with the truth' (Preface 2). To this end Irenaeus cited texts at length, interrupting his reporting of them by sentences of commentary – quotation and commentary are difficult to distinguish. Still, in this way the Bishop of Gaul handed on the outline of a great system and various lesser texts on its periphery. As early as in the Preface he attributed these extracts from sources to pupils of a Christian theologian named Ptolemy, who lived in Rome in the middle of the second century, and reported that this school claimed its origin from another urban Roman Christian theologian named Valentinus, though in reality it derived from people who called themselves 'knowers', 'gnostics' (*Refutation* I, 31, 3, etc.). Irenaeus likewise made the storical and intellectual connections between the 'knowers' and the disciples of the Roman teacher, the 'Valentinians', the subject of his books. He presented the magician Simon from Flavia Neapolis, present-day Nablus, in Samaria/ Palestine, as the founder of gnosis, 'its source and root' (*Refutation* I, 22, 2). Irenaeus set against what he thought to be the confused views of his opponents, the morals of some of whom were deeply corrupt, the simple, comprehensible faith which all could follow, orientated on the criterion of truth that had come down in the church from the apostles to those in positions of responsibility in the community of his time.

Clement of Alexandria

I have already mentioned the Christian teacher Titus Flavius Clemens from Alexandria. He must have been writing about two decades after Irenaeus. The title of his main work, in seven volumes, already indicates that it belongs to the genre of mixed writings, the so-called 'miscellanea': *Carpets of Descriptions which Relate to Knowledge in Respect of the True Philosophy*. In keeping with this literary genre, Christian doctrine is unfolded in that work in a colourful mixture and not in any strict order. But time and again Clement is concerned with right 'knowledge' as opposed to a 'knowledge wrongly so-called': 'Obscurity and imagination have given philosophy a bad name, and the same thing has happened to knowledge as a result of false knowledge which bears the same name' (*Carpets* II, 5, 5). However, in his *Carpets* he does not offer a systematic refutation of the 'baneful knowledge of these people who are wrongly called knowers'. Rather, he promises this at a later point in time, 'so that combating them, which cannot be done with a few words, does not disrupt my investigation and interrupt the present train of thought, in which we want to show that only that gnostic is truly holy and pious who is really so in accordance with the criterion of the church' (*Carpets* VII, 41, 3). Consequently, in contrast to Irenaeus, Clement quotes only shorter passages from writings to which he attributes this false knowledge. His quotations from Aristotle or Plato far outweigh his quotations from writings which are still attributed to 'gnosis'. We have a further writing by Clement under the title *Excerpts from Theodotus and the So-Called 'Eastern' Teaching at the Time of Valentinus,* which was evidently not destined for publication in its present form, because in the form of a collection of material without introduction or conclusion it mixes up reports of teaching which is likewise in the tradition of Valentinus, who taught in Rome, with commentaries by Clement. This comparatively short text contains a large number of original texts of 'knowledge'.

Hippolytus of Rome

Around twenty years later, the third relevant author, Hippolytus of Rome, wrote another *Refutation of all Heresies* (*Refutatio Omnium Haeresium*), only fragments of which have been handed down. Books V to IX depict 33 groups which modern scholars designate 'gnostics'. However, according to Hippolytus virtually only the members of a single group, the 'Naassenes', called themselves 'knowers': 'They take this name from the Hebrew word "Naas", snake. Later they called themselves "knowers", since they claimed that they alone knew the depths of wisdom' (*Refutation* V, 6, 3f.; cf. also 23, 3). The other groups are introduced under names, some of which were presumably given to them by opponents to describe their teaching, but some of which also describe their understanding of themselves or are even designations that they gave themselves: the snake people ('Naassenes'), the 'foreigners' (Perates) or the 'Seth people'. Alongside this the teaching of individual theologians like Simon, Valentinus, Secundus, Ptolemy, Heracleon, Marcus and Colorbasus is presented. Unfortunately, however, Hippolytus gives only a few details which would help us in putting them in a historical context.

Hippolytus reports more and quotes less: 'The teaching of the Sethians seems to us to have been sufficiently explained. But if anyone wants to learn their whole action and activity, let him read the book which bears the title "The Paraphrase of Seth" ' (*Refutation* V, 22). However, his work, too, quotes some important original sources. Hippolytus is firmly convinced that the relevant groups have got involved in Greek philosophy to their detriment; they have misunderstood its foundations, thrown it together clumsily and in this way have both fallen away from the true faith and got bogged down in completely illogical constructions (*Refutation* I, Preface 8f.).

Origen

Probably shortly after this, and long before the middle of the third century, the first really highly educated Christian theologian and polymath Origen – his Christian parents had given their child the pagan name 'offspring of Horus' – when composing his 22-volume commentary on the New Testament Gospel of John took issue with a comparable work by a prominent 'Valentinian', an adherent of the Roman teacher Valentinus, who has already been mentioned. The explanation of the Fourth Gospel written by Heracleon (we have almost 50 fragments), which is quoted by Origen at length but not always critically, must come from the second half of the second century AD. Almost nothing is known of the circumstances of this author Heracleon, but we can recognize from the fragments that Heracleon was evidently the first Christian author to expound the Gospel verse by verse in accordance with the philological methods of commentary customary in antiquity: in the fragments we find above all explanations of factual matters (*historikon*) which sometimes go very thoroughly into philological problems and thus presuppose an explanation of words (*glossematikon*), and grammatical and rhetorical exegesis (*technikon*), even if few such passages have been handed on by Origen. So the author Heracleon, who is usually assigned to 'gnosis', is the first Christian writer whose comprehensive exegesis of a New Testament writing has come down to us, albeit in fragmentary form.

Epiphanius of Salamis

The fifth and last author, Epiphanius of Salamis, metropolitan of Cyprus in late antiquity, hands on a whole series of Greek source texts and critical reflections on these sources in a work which bears the attractive title *Medicine Chest against the Heresies* (*Panarion adversus haereses*), composed in the 370s. These texts include some passages of the original Greek text of Irenaeus which is otherwise lost. Picking up a passage from the Bible ('There are 60 queens and 80 concubines', Song of Solomon 6.8), the pugnacious theologian discusses 20 'pre-Christian' and 60 'Christian' heresies in his work, the most comprehensive encyclopaedia in Christian antiquity to be directed against 'heretics'. In his preface the monk and bishop excuses his vigorous language and polemic, which he attributes to his 'annoyance about the sects' and the attempt to protect readers from these dangerous movements (*Medicine Chest*, Preface to Book I, 2, 3). Epiphanius put around 20 groups which scholars today assign to 'knowledge' among the 60 sects 'which bear the name of Christ but do not have his faith'. However, he called only a single group out of these 60 'gnostic', 'knower' (although he believed that he knew that the adherents of Valentinus also gave themselves this name, *Medicine Chest* II, 31, 1, 1 and 5). In his long section on the 'knowers', Epiphanius reported that in Egypt these people would be called 'Stratiotikoi' and 'Phibionitai', in Upper Egypt 'Sekundianoi', in other places 'Zakchaioi' and by yet others 'Koddianoi' or 'Borboritai' (*Medicine Chest* II, 26, 1–2). Not only present-day readers find these names quite remarkable; thanks to such monstrosities Epiphanius, too, could be sure of the deterrent effect of his account – precisely as he had announced in the Preface. We can only conjecture about the meaning of such designations, which the monk, who originally came from Palestine, will have picked up on visits to fellow monks in Egypt. 'Stratiotikoi' means 'the warlike', and may be a self-designation of a group of self-confident Christians or even an ironic name given to them by others. 'Phibiontai' may allude to a name of the Egyptian God Hermes Thoth ('Phibi', *Katalog der astrologischen Handschriften* 1, 167) and should then perhaps be translated 'the Hermes people', an allusion to the astrological competences of the group. The adherents of some Secundus must have been called 'Secundians'; here it must remain open whether the Valentinian mentioned in Irenaeus was Secundus (*Refutation* I, 11, 2); the same goes for 'Zakchaioi', which presumably means 'adherents of one Zacchaeus' (unknown to us) or is an allusion to the original meaning of this Hebrew name ('the pure'). If the 'knowers' were also called 'Sokratitai' in Egypt, this will have been a variant on 'Sokratistai', a term of mockery used in classical Greek of 'imitators of Socrates', i.e. those who in their form of life recalled this rather curious philosopher – or even followed his style. Epiphanius attempts to explain two names himself: he derives 'Koddianoi' from the word *koddah*, which in the dialogue of his home region means 'jar' and is also attested as a Greek loan word; he says that the people are called 'jar people' because no one wants to eat with them and drink from the same jar (*Medicine Chest* II, 26, 3 and 5). The angry bishop – like modern lexicons – derives 'Borboritai' from the Greek word *borborodes*, which means 'dirty': 'the dirty ones'. But regardless of who or what these 'knowers' were, whether 'dirty' or 'Socratic', it becomes crystal clear that Christian theologians like Epiphanius were often merely gathering unexamined rumours, and it requires a great deal of effort to get precise information from this mixture of information and calumny. What is still most interesting about this curious medley is the report that in Egypt people whom Epiphanius assigned to 'knowledge' were mockingly denounced as copies of the Greek sage Socrates. Such polemic points to the kind of claim that we also have reported in other sources about 'knowers': these people attempted to present themselves as especially shrewd and wise Christians.

Epiphanius himself reported that as a young man on a visit
to Egypt he was informed about their teachings by beautiful
women who belonged to this group, but that he had not
been convinced. Rather, he writes, he reported everything
to the bishops, and as a result 80 adherents who had lived
in secret within the Christian church had been expelled
from a particular place – unfortunately we are given no
names (*Medicine Chest* II, 26, 17, 1–6). This information,
too, is of great interest, because it shows that these
'knowers' belonged to the normal Christian community
and evidently had drawn no attention to themselves until
the activities of the heresy-hunter Epiphanius. The bishop
also noted with similar indignation that everyone called
members of such sects Christians without making any
distinction, although after all they were not in the truth
(29, 6, 6).

2. Authors critical of 'gnosis', who offer 'reports on heretics' (heresiologists)

There is also important information in early Christian
theologians who made the combating of 'heretics' their
task. As they called their opponents 'heretics' (*hairetikoi* in
Greek), in modern research too they tend to be called
'heresiologists'. Of course we must always check the value
of information that we gain from this material over against
the overall polemical tendency that we find. Here in
addition to the authors Irenaeus of Lyons, Clement
of Alexandria, Hippolytus of Rome and Epiphanius of
Salamis, who have already been mentioned, we must
consider above all Justin, who worked in the city of Rome,
and Tertullian, who worked in Carthage.

Justin, the philosopher and martyr

Justin, who was already called 'philosopher and martyr' in
antiquity, came from Palestine, more precisely from
present-day Nablus, the ancient Shechem/Flavia Neapolis.

After studying philosophy he lived and taught in the
imperial capital, Rome, around the middle of the second
century as a free teacher of Christianity, and wore the
garment characteristic of philosophers, the philosopher's
cloak. He was executed for his Christian faith
around 165. He composed two works in his defence (Greek
'Apologies'), presumably out of his teaching activity, which
must have consisted of lengthy lectures to which people
had free admission. In these Apologies the philosopher
wanted to argue for the toleration of Christianity by the
state and to refute the most important public charges
against the new religion. Unfortunately his real literary
controversy with the 'heretics', entitled 'Compendium
against the Heretics', was already lost in antiquity and its
contents can no longer really be reconstructed. However,
we do learn some interesting details from the First Apology,
composed around AD 150, about two Christian teachers
who like Justin came from Samaria in Palestine: the
magician Simon, who is also mentioned in the Acts of
the Apostles in the New Testament, with his Roman
community (Acts 8.9–24 and *Apology* I, 26, 2f.), and his
disciple Menander (26,4). Since then, both of them have
been reckoned among the early gnostics. Justin also
mentions Marcion, a shipowner from Sinope on the Black
Sea, who was a contemporary of his in Rome and later
founded a counter-church. Marcion must have been
treated at greater length in the lost Compendium. Justin's
information is important above all for determining from
what point in time and in what contexts the movement that
we usually call 'knowledge' arose.

Tertullian

Quintus Septimius Florens Tertullianus, Tertullian for
short, was the first Christian writer in antiquity to write in
Latin. He must have lived between 160 and 220. Possibly
Tertullian's father was a senior officer in the army; at all
events he gave his son an admirable education and a
certain social status. Linguistically, too, Tertullian's writings

reveal great knowledge: he used forceful expressions in the vernacular, gave them point with his sharp but witty polemic, and enriched the language with new technical terms. Thus he invented the Latin form of the word 'trinity', *trinitas*, in order to denote the fact that the one God reveals himself in three persons: Father, Son and Holy Spirit. The impression that here a thinker living in Carthage, the capital of a self-consciously independent province of the empire, represents this particularly independent North African spirit down to details of language, has been formulated time and again and is certainly not completely inaccurate. As with Justin, his first writings are devoted to the defence of Christianity against the accusations of his non-Christian contemporaries. However, the writings which are particularly relevant to research into 'knowledge' are those in which with witty but sharp polemic, completely in line with what were then the modern stylistic laws of the so-called second sophistry, in admirable Latin Tertullian attacks individual 'heretics' and whole 'groups of heretics'. While one work, *Against the Valentinians*, ironically attacks the teaching of 'gnostics' who claimed to be disciples of the Roman teacher Valentinus (*Adversus Valentinianos, c.* 206/207) and the work *Against Marcion* attacks in five books theses and the edition of the Bible by the Roman teacher (*Adversus Marcionem, c.* 207/208), the works *On the Flesh of Christ* (*De carne Christi, c.* AD 206) and *On the Resurrection of the Dead* (*De resurrectione mortuorum, c.* AD 211) discuss controversial theological points in a way which is generally directed against the opponents mentioned.

Further authors

Of course, scattered source material from reports on 'knowledge' can also be found in many other early Christian theologians, for example in the Syrian teacher Ephraem, who lived and worked from AD 306 to 373 in Nisibis (Nusaybin in present-day Turkey) and Edessa (Urfa in present-day Turkey), or the famous North African theologian and bishop Augustine (AD 354–430). Thus for example it is possible to reconstruct from a relevant writing of Augustine ('Against the Letter that they [the Manichaeans] call "Letter of Fundamentals"', AD 396) and other scattered texts the wording and general argument of the 'Letter of Fundamentals', the *Epistula Fundamenti* of the Manichaeans of North Africa.

Usually Islamic scholars and their works, which are particularly important for the reconstruction of the Manichaean system of religion, are overlooked. Perhaps best known is still the Arabic polymath Abu r-Riaḥān Muhammad ibn Ahmad al-Bīrūnī (973–1048). Of course his astrological-astronomical, geodetic, mineralogical or pharmacological writings are not relevant to our subject, but the 'Remaining Traces of Past Generations', a history of the world from the perspective of an astronomer, which Eduard Sachau edited under the title *Chronology of Oriental Peoples* in 1878 and translated into English in 1879, is. Although al-Bīrūnī has no eye for the teaching of Manichaeism, he provides very thorough and careful information about the history and life of this form of religion.

3. Original 'gnostic' texts, above all in Coptic

Particularly in the twentieth century, the new discoveries of complete writings which can be assigned to 'gnosis' has revolutionized research, because now as well as the more or less extensive quotations in the writings of opponents we also have the original texts without any polemical commentary. This group of sources includes above all the famous library of thirteen codices with just under fifty writings on more than a thousand pages which was found in Nag Hammadi in Upper Egypt in 1945/6. The Manichaean texts discovered at Medinet Madi are also to be included in this group of sources. The fact that these writings have largely been preserved not in Greek but in Coptic dialects indicates that they were also disseminated among simpler circles of the population of Egypt – after all, the Coptic dialects are a written vernacular which developed from New Egyptian as the language used in the everyday life of the population.

Codices Askewianus and Brucianus

As early as the end of the eighteenth century there was a fourth-century codex with Coptic texts in the British Museum in London named 'Codex Askewianus' after one Askew, its former owner. It contains two long writings, usually assigned to 'gnosis', which are difficult to understand. Their original titles are unknown, but the whole manuscript is usually called 'Pistis Sophia', i.e. 'Faith – Wisdom', because in the middle of the manuscript a reference has been inserted to a corresponding title and the first writing reports the experiences of a figure with the same name. However, at another point the manuscript also has the title 'Books of the Redeemer'. It is certain that these Coptic texts have been translated from the Greek. As they are based on the Egyptian calendar, the writings must have been composed in Egypt or otherwise worked over thoroughly when being translated. In its present form the text is so complicated that one scholar has spoken of 'an old man's gnosticism' (Harnack, *Über das gnostische Buch Pistis Sophia*, 1891, 97). However, the non-reader-friendly form also shows that the writing was worked over time and again and was a much-used text.

In the middle of the nineteenth century the Bodleian Library in Oxford bought a comparable codex from the heirs of the famous Scottish traveller James Bruce, the 'Codex Brucianus', which presumably comes from the same period. This manuscript, too, contains a long text without a title; its beginning runs 'This is the book of the knowledges' – the Greek word *gnosis* also appears in the Coptic text – 'of the invisible God corresponding to the hidden mysteries which show the way to the elect generation' (257, 5–7). However, the text is usually called the 'Books of Jeû', after a figure who in the text is called 'the true God' and is presented as being brought forth from the

supreme deity (260, 23f.). Along with related forms like
'Jao' and 'Jabe', 'Jeû' is evidently a pronunciation of the
Jewish name of God YHWH, written in the four consonants
of the tetragrammaton. The so-called 'magical papyri',
instructions for magical actions and sayings which people
in antiquity could purchase, offer all kinds of examples of
such forms of words (Index VI to the Greek magical papyri,
222f.). In such literature people evidently used the Jewish
name of God, the pronunciation of which was really
forbidden to pious Jews, because it was felt to be powerful
and numinous. In the writing from the Codex Brucianus
the Jewish divine name is a term which was in any case
associated with God in the Jewish-Christian tradition, and is
used to denote a form of this supreme God closely
connected with the supreme God. The two codices also
have further texts, shorter and longer, including interesting prayer texts that indicate something of the intensive
piety of the people who read such texts. The first two
strophes of a six-strophe prayer from the Codex Brucianus
are:

> 'Hear me as I praise you,
>   mystery existing before all that is incomprehensible and
>   infinite,
>   hear me as I praise you,
>   O mystery which shone forth in its mystery,
>   That the mystery existing from the beginning might
>   become complete ...'
> (333, 3–8).

Since the two codices were initially the only extant
original sources accessible to scholars, until the great
discoveries of texts in the twentieth century they misled
them into seeing 'gnosis' exclusively as a conglomerate of
confused mythologoumena. Only through the new
discoveries has the intellectual claim of such writings also
become clearer; some of this claim has been lost in the
Coptic vernacular simply as a result of clumsy translation.

The Berlin Codex

Finally, the early textual discoveries also include the remains of a papyrus booklet which the Berlin Coptologist Carl Schmidt (1868–1938) discovered in Egypt in 1896 and gave to the Berlin Museums, where the codex has since then been catalogued as 'Papyrus Berolinensis 8502'. It was purchased from an antique dealer, so we do not know where it was found; presumably it dates from the fifth century. The later leather cover bears the owner's mark of an abbot by the name of Zechariah, so it can be conjectured that the texts were in a monastic library of late antiquity. Because of various problems of a technical and personal nature the text, which today is known above all by the name 'Codex Berolinensis gnosticus', was inaccessible for 60 years: among other things, the manuscript of the first edition by Schmidt, which is handwritten and therefore exists only in a single copy, was destroyed by water in a fire at the printers. Only after the Second World War, in 1955, did the first printing of an edition appear which has been revised several times by the Berlin Coptologist Hans-Martin Schenke. The booklet contains four works: 'The Gospel according to Mary', 'The Secret Writing of John', 'The Wisdom of Jesus Christ' and 'The Acts of Peter'.

The 'Gospel according to Mary' (EvMar) is attested not only in the Berlin Codex but also in two papyrus fragments (Papyrus Oxyrhynchus 3525 and Rylands 463). The title seems to indicate that this is a supplement to the four Gospels 'according to Matthew, Mark, Luke and John' which are canonized in the New Testament. But in truth the fragmentary text consists of two units which were perhaps once independent and now have also been linked in a literary fashion: a first part contains an exchange between the Redeemer and disciples about the theological problem of the connection between matter and sin; a second part hands on a discussion between Mary Magdalene and the disciples. Peter asks Mary, 'whom the Redeemer loved more than the other women' (BG 10, 2f.), to hand on to them the words of the Redeemer which they

did not hear from him themselves. In a later section there
is a description of a kind of ascension of the soul of Mary
which she undertakes together with the Redeemer (17,
9f.). Thus the text presupposes that Mary received special
revelations; one of the disciples even says in the Gospel that
their authenticity was disputed: 'I at least do not believe
that the Redeemer said that' (13f.).

The 'Secret Writing of John', in Greek the 'Apocryphon
of John' (AJ), is attested not only in the Berlin Codex but
also in the Nag Hammadi Library in three versions (NHC
II, 1; III, 1 and IV, 1). However, these four texts differ
considerably from one another: NHC II, 1 and IV, 1 are
witnesses to a longer version; NHC III, 1 and the Berlin
Codex are witnesses to a text which is shorter by a third.
Moreover, in his *Refutation*, Irenaeus of Lyons quotes a
short text which is closely related to the 'Secret Writing' (I,
29, 1–4). The complicated history of the text is now seen
like this. At the beginning of the third century a very short
original, known to Irenaeus, was expanded. This version
has come down to us in the form of the shorter recension
of a later Coptic translation of the early fourth century. At
some point during the third century the shorter version was
again expanded, and this longer version, too, was translated into Coptic at the beginning of the following century.
It is clear from this extremely complicated history that the
'Secret Writing' was not regarded as a fixed, sacred text;
rather, it was continually worked over, and the result was
also evidently never subjected to a final redaction which
once again critically checked the meaning of the often
expanded text. Nor do the translators who translated the
Greek texts into Coptic always seem to have understood
precisely what the original meaning of a passage was. The
book begins with an appearance of Christ, who teaches the
sorrowful and brooding (apostle) John about 'what was
and is to be', so that he knows 'the invisible and the visible
and ... the perfect man' (BG 22, 4–10). Further divine
figures exist alongside the quite unimaginable and invisible
supreme God: first an image of the supreme God by the
name 'Barbelo' or 'the first man' (on this see below,

pp. 44f.). The text describes how further divine figures arise from the supreme God, which it calls 'eternities' (Greek 'aeons') to show that they are partial aspects of the one God which for logical reasons are depicted in the form of separate personalities. These partial aspects of God are at the same time the heavenly models of earthly realities – just as, say, the first human being is the heavenly model of earthly human beings; of course the thought here is utterly Platonic, although ancient Platonists would presumably have been very surprised at the remarkable names and ideas. Despite all appearances to the contrary, the system developed here of one God in a multiplicity of aspects which tends towards infinity is monotheistic, not polytheistic. This fact is expressed in the 'Secret Writing' with the Platonic image of a spring (BG 26, 19–21): just as water streams out of the spring and yet the spring always remains a spring and at the same time the water streaming out always remains water, so the supreme God knows himself in the 'eternities' which surround him (27, 1–4) and which, after all, he himself is. With such a doctrine of God an attempt is evidently being made to make the talk of one God, which Christianity had taken over from Judaism, competitive with the ideas of popular philosophy and also at the same time to incorporate the figure of Jesus Christ quite naturally into the process of the self-explication of the one deity. The basic tone of the 'Secret Writing' remains that of popular Platonism, when a heavenly model is constructed for the stories of the creation of the world and human beings that are handed down in the Old Testament, and the partial aspects of God, i.e. his 'eternities', are permitted what the members of the community want for themselves: the knowledge of the truth (BG 32, 14–19). The number and names of the eternities seem random to the modern reader, but they are not: an effort was made to use the numbers which were sacred and significant to the educated world (4, 7 and 12) and to introduce into the system as many biblical names and terms as possible for knowledge and the capacity for knowledge, along with mysterious angelic names from the Jewish tradition. In addition to the fall of the first human couple in paradise reported in the Bible, a myth of the fall of an 'eternity' of God, i.e. a partial aspect of God, is constructed: the 'eternity wisdom' falls and creates a defective creator God named Ialdaboath, who likewise provides himself with partial divine aspects and angelic beings. Whereas the mythological narrative merely elaborates in a very colourful way what was related in contemporary Judaism about the fall of the angels from heavenly glory (in the New Testament see only Rev. 12.9), the text also gives the educated reader an explanation of why partial aspects of God could become remote from God himself – to use the Platonic image, how water from the spring could have become cloudy. The text also explains how emotional affects like desire and anger have led to the aspects of God becoming independent and alien to God. For present-day taste this explanation may be a long way from what is usually understood by Christianity, but it is an attempt to reconstruct a divine prehistory and heavenly model for the biblical stories of the fall of humankind which would make the fall plausible to contemporaries educated in popular Platonism. The 'Secret Writing of John' is not even original at this point: ancient Judaism had already interpreted talk of 'sons of God' walking on earth in the first book of the Bible (Gen. 6.2) to mean that emotional affects like lust and envy made the divine angelic beings fall from heaven so that evil came into the world (Life of Adam and Eve 12–17 or Ethiopian Enoch 7–10, 18f. and 65–9). However, according to the 'Secret Writing' the imperfect creator god Ialdabaoth reflects, and thus various divine powers together with him create the first human being Adam as the image of the original 'perfect human being' (BG 48, 11–50, 14). Nor did the 'Secret Writing' invent such an interpretation of the biblical creation story, which is again surprising at first sight; it too was already widespread in Judaism and avoided the impression which might be gained from reading the Bible that the supreme God was a kind of craftsman who had 'plucked' the first human being from the ground. The 'Secret Writing' then also explains

why human beings live in a body which has fallen victim to
death and why they are no longer capable of 'knowledge' –
because of their creator's envy of their capabilities (BG 55,
3–13; 58, 10–14). And it ends with detailed instructions
about how one can escape this misery, gain 'knowledge',
and again enter the heavenly reality. However, there are
three groups of human beings: those for whom this is
possible in this life through a heavenly gift; those who
attain knowledge and are saved only after death, and those
about whom it is utterly unclear whether they will enter the
heavenly glory.

The 'Wisdom of Jesus Christ', commonly also called the
'Sophia of Jesus Christ' (SJC) after the Greek, begins with
a revelation discourse of Jesus which he addresses to twelve
disciples and seven women on a mountain after the
resurrection (BG 77, 9–16). The Redeemer promises to
communicate to his hearers things that they do not yet
know and about which the philosophers have offered
conflicting conjectures: 'Who God is or of what nature he
is' (80, 10–12). What is then said about God corresponds
more clearly than in the 'Secret Writing' to what one could
hear in any Middle-Platonic philosophical school – though
in a rather chaotic order: God is immortal, eternal, without
beginning and name, not in human form, imperishable
and inconceivable, good and perfect (84, 1–87, 8). Only in
the subsequent passages are there remarks about further
divine forces, above all about 'a first immortal male-female
human being' (94, 9–11). In this way again models are
constructed in the heavenly world of earthly phenomena,
human beings and even of Jesus of Nazareth. In the Nag
Hammadi Library, not only has a version of the Wisdom of
Jesus Christ been discovered which is very similar to the
Berlin text (NHC III, 4; cf. also a papyrus leaf with Greek
texts, Papyrus Oxyrhynchus 1081), but also a writing which
is related in many passages, the 'Letter of Eugnostos', the
original title of which is 'Eugnostos, the Blessed' (NHC III,
3). One of the central differences between the 'Wisdom'
and the letter is the lack of allusions to biblical scenes and
figures in the Letter of Eugnostos. But in the letter, too,

there is a divine figure named 'Redeemer' who is part of the divine fullness. The context makes it clear that here the thought is not of one of the Greek gods who could be called 'redeemer' in antiquity – thus Asclepius is called 'redeemer of the sick' and Zeus, the father of the gods, is regularly invoked as 'redeemer' – but of a heavenly model of the earthly figure of Christ. That is clear simply from the fact that he derives from another divine figure, 'the Son of man' (NHC III, 3, 81, 21–82, 7). Thus the authors of the 'Letter of Eugnostos' have attempted to use the various titles customary in the church for a number of divine figures and thus – like the 'Secret Writing' – to distinguish as many authorities and aspects as possible within the one Jewish Christian God in order to remain competitive in the religious market of antiquity. Consequently it would be better not to describe the 'Letter of Eugnostos', which presumably represents an earlier stage of textual history than the 'Wisdom', as a non-Christian writing; a whole series of ancient Christian texts are written in such a way as to avoid extensive allusions to biblical passages and names in order to make them more accessible to non-Christians.

Finally, the title 'Act of Peter' harbours part of the so-called Acts of Peter, a romance read throughout ancient Christianity, which relates further travels and miracles of Peter over and above those in the New Testament Acts of the Apostles. This text has nothing to do with the rich mythological constructions of the three writings mentioned previously; rather, it belongs to the romance-like Christian entertainment literature of antiquity and is evidence that the person who had the codex copied and who used it was interested in simple pious entertainment as well as in deeper 'knowledge' about the nature of God and human beings. The passage is meant to show that bodily suffering can also have a good side if it helps to preserve the virginity of a woman. That restraint towards sexuality is called for in the 'Acts' will have delighted the monk who read the book, as will the not very friendly verdict on the earthly body in the 'Secret Writing'. However, the most varied intellectual currents in antiquity were agreed on this somewhat critical attitude to the body and corporeality.

The Nag Hammadi Library

The history of the discovery of the Nag Hammadi Library in 1945/6 is at least as exciting as the content of the find itself. We can reconstruct it from the reports of an Egyptian fellah involved in the find who lived until the 1980s. He later reported how together with his brother he discovered the papyri in a large earthenware jar in one of the many caves in a limestone rock near present-day Hamra Dom in Upper Egypt. The nearest major settlement on the Nile is Nag Hammadi, which is also a railway station. The find is somewhat imprecisely called the 'Nag Hammadi Library' after this little town, around ten kilometres from the site of the real discovery. The fellahin did not hand over what they found to a museum but attempted to make money out of it, so that parts appeared on the market only gradually. The brothers' mother is said to have burned at least one codex in the oven because she feared that the old texts, which no one in the family was in a position to read, might perhaps have dangerous effects. As the two brothers were entangled in a feud, they deposited the manuscripts with a Coptic priest, whose brother-in-law in October 1946 sold a first codex to the Coptic Museum in Old Cairo, which today is numbered Codex III. The Coptologist and historian of religion Jean Doresse had a look at it there. When Doresse had recognized the significance and character of the text, in 1948 he published a first reference to the find. Meanwhile a Belgian antique dealer had purchased a further codex in Cairo, taken it abroad, and offered it for sale in both New York and Paris. Finally, a foundation acquired the codex for the Carl Gustav Jung Institute in Zurich in 1951 through the mediation of Gilles Quispel and with the active support of sponsors. The papyrus leaves were to be a birthday present for the famous psychologist and were given the name 'Jung Codex' (today Codex I). After Jung's death in 1961 there was a dispute over the

ownership, so the pages were not handed over by the new
owners to the Coptic Museum in Old Cairo until 1975, after
a first critical edition. The other volumes of the find
reached a Cypriot antique dealer in Cairo from the hands
of the Coptic priest by various intermediaries and were
then taken over in exchange for compensation by the
Department of Antiquities, because it was feared that these
parts of the find would also be taken abroad. Jean Doresse
published a first report on these codices, too (according to
the present-day numbering Codex II, IV–XI and the
remains of Codices I, XII and XIII), as early as 1949.
However, then, because the rights of ownership had not
been settled, the texts remained for a number of years in a
sealed chest. After Nasser's revolution in 1956 they were
declared national property and likewise handed over to the
Coptic Museum in Old Cairo. All the extant codices of
the Nag Hammadi Library can be seen in this collection on
request. Of the 1945 find, eleven complete books and
fragments of two others, amounting to well over 1000
written pages, have been preserved. The extant books
were originally bound in elegant goatskin covers with
simple geometrical patterns. A loop on the cover and, in
individual cases, further loops on the back made it possible
to shut the book with leather thongs and tie it up into a
convenient, protected package. Meanwhile, to aid conservation the beautiful leather bindings have long since been
detached, and all the leaves have been put individually
between pieces of glass. When the leather bindings were
removed, among other things, remnants of business papers
and correspondence from the middle of the fourth century
were found, so that on the basis of further indications the
script and binding of the thirteen books could be dated to
this time. Since there is mention in the papers used for the
binding of a letter to a monk from a famous Orthodox
monastery named 'Chenoboskeia' or 'Chenoboskion',
'Goose Meadow' (Letter 153 from the cover of Codex XI),
which is not even ten kilometres from the place where the
library was found, time and again it has been conjectured
that the books were prepared or at least purchased for a

monastery, and at a later point in time were removed from the monastery as heretical writings and buried in a jar.

This conjecture is supported by an interesting parallel tradition to a text from Nag Hammadi: a pseudonymous writing containing general rules about wisdom has been preserved in the library, the title of which attributes its composition to one Silvanus (probably he is anachronistically meant to be the companion of the apostle Paul, cf. 2 Cor. 1.19): 'The Teachings of Silvanus' (NHC VII, 4). In this text not only is there polemic against certain positions on the creation of the world which occur in other works from Nag Hammadi (116, 5–10); one passage has also been preserved on a sheet of parchment in London (Or. 6003) under the name of the founder of Egyptian monasticism in the church, 'Father Antony' (*c.* AD 251–356) and in a further document of Egyptian monasticism. So we can well imagine that individual works from the Nag Hammadi Library were read not just with abhorrence but with spiritual gain in Egyptian monastic circles. Such observations are not of course in themselves reliable indications of the original age of the writings; here the dates put forward in current research vary a great deal. There is real certainty only about the very few writings which have also been preserved in other contexts.

The history of editions of the Nag Hammadi Library is almost as complicated as the story of its discovery. The first edition of the text of a writing from the so-called 'Jung Codex' appeared in Cairo in 1956 and a single volume of an extensive facsimile edition which had been planned. Because of a rather unfortunate fixed assignation of editions to individual scholars and the difficult political circumstances, initially only individual tractates from the find in Cairo and the writings of the Zurich manuscript appeared. A decisive turning-point came about only in 1966. At the Messina Congress of that year, which has already been mentioned, the American New Testament scholar James M. Robinson, also an expert on religion, brought together a team of editors and translators which was to publish a bilingual edition of the Coptic text with

English translation in close collaboration with the Institute for Antiquity and Christianity in Claremont, California. Moreover, a facsimile edition did appear in twelve volumes between 1972 and 1979, so that now the whole find is available for further research to all interested parties – in contrast to other great discoveries of texts in the twentieth century like the famous Qumran texts from the wilderness of Judaea. Meanwhile in Germany above all Alexander Böhlig, Martin Krause and the New Testament scholars Gesine Schenke, Hans-Martin Schenke and Hans-Gebhard Bethge, working in the former German Democratic Republic, have been continuing their editions. The last three scholars belong to the Berlin Working Party for Coptic-Gnostic Writings at the Berlin Humboldt University, which has prepared the first complete scholarly translation into German; it has just been published. A further complete edition has been got under way by Jacques-É. Ménard; already most of the writings of the find have appeared in this series, for which the Laval University in Québec, Canada, has taken responsibility.

If we make a list of the 13 codices with 52 writings (see also the chart on pp. 123–6), it is striking, first, that a series of writings are represented several times in the Nag Hammadi Library, namely the 'Secret Writing of John', i.e. the 'Apocryphon of John', three times (NHC II, 1; III, 1; IV, 1; also BG 2), and twice each the 'Gospel of Truth' (NHC I, 3; XII, 2), the 'Gospel of the Egyptians' (NHC III, 2; IV, 2), an untitled writing usually called 'On the Origin of the World' (NHC II, 5; VIII, 2), and finally the so-called 'Letter to Eugnostos' (NHC III, 3; V, 1). Moreover, it is striking that very different literary genres are represented within the one library and their ordering seems quite random. Above all, all the genres which also occur in the canonical New Testament of the Christian church are represented. The Coptic writings seem to allude to these models: thus there is a '*Gospel* according to Thomas' (NHC II, 2) and a '*Gospel* according to Philip' (NHC II, 3). Both writings are formally orientated on a specific form of the New Testament tradition, the so-called 'Sayings Gospel', a collection of sayings of Jesus. The authors of the canonical Gospels of Matthew and Luke had such a collection before them and it can be reconstructed with some degree of reliability from these texts (the so-called 'Q' source). By contrast, the writing from the library which bears the modern title 'Gospel of Truth' (NHC I, 3; XII, 2) is more of a sermon, and has understood the words 'gospel of truth' which form the beginning of the text quite literally: 'the good news of the truth'. The real title of the so-called 'Gospel of the Egyptians' (NHC III, 2; IV, 2) is 'The Holy Book of the Great, Invisible Spirit' and is put at the end of the work, in accordance with ancient practice. Only later has a passage from the beginning ('the holy book of the Egyptians', III, 2, 40, 12) been interpreted as 'Gospel of the Egyptians'.

Among the letters in the library are two which are attributed to apostles: a 'Letter of James' (NHC I, 2) and a 'Letter of Peter to Philip' (NHC VIII, 2); there are also letters to a certain Rheginus (NHC I, 4) and a Eugnostos (NHC III, 3; VI, 1). However, only the second title is original: all the others are inferred and reconstructed. The epistolary character almost always fades into the background in favour of a didactic-discursive form. The Nag Hammadi Library contains no private letters, but doctrinal tractates which are superficially stylized as letters in order to assimilate them to the biblical model. Similarly, in the collection there is also a parallel to the New Testament Acts of the Apostles: the 'Acts of Peter and the Twelve Apostles' (NHC VI, 1). Here, as in the New Testament, there is a narrative about a mythical journey/ voyage, but in contrast to the biblical model it is not concrete, and the geography is inaccurate. At the end of the journey Jesus reveals himself and sends his disciples into the world (NHC VI, 1, 9, 1–12, 20).

The literary genre of the 'apocalypses' ('revelations') occupies a good deal of space in the library; this is a literary genre taken over into Christianity from Judaism in which the present is interpreted in an authoritative religious way and the future is announced. Thus an 'Apocalypse of Paul' (NHC V, 2) has been found which broadly depicts what is only hinted at in the authentic letters of the apostle: there Paul writes that someone he knows – presumably himself – was once transported to the third sphere of heaven and 'heard inexpressible words which no human being can utter' (2 Cor. 12.2–4). The apocalypse from the Nag Hammadi find makes Paul travel through the third sphere of heaven to the fourth (19, 22f.) and records what he saw there: the judgement of the dead. The apostle travels on from the fifth through the sixth to the seventh sphere of heaven, where he sees 'an old man' with white garments on a throne (22, 24–30). This man gives Paul authority to lead out those imprisoned in the world of the dead – and thus bestows on him a function which in the view of the majority of the Christian theologians of the time was that of Christ himself. But from the fact that Paul penetrates further, to the tenth sphere of heaven, it becomes evident that this old man – contrary to some Jewish doctrines about seven spheres of heaven – cannot yet be the supreme God and Father. There he meets only his fellow spirits (25, 5f.) – unfortunately we are not told what or who else is there. The library also contains two different 'Apocalypses of James' (NHC V, 3–4), the first of which has the character of a dialogue between James and Jesus, whereas the second is stylized as a farewell discourse of James. In contrast to the writings of the canonical New Testament James is characterized as the beloved disciple of Jesus, and Jesus promises him 'revelations of such things as neither the heavens nor their archons have known' (NHC V, 4, 56, 18–21). At the end there is an account of the martyrdom of James, certain features of which recall other ancient accounts of the end of the life of this brother of Jesus, who after Jesus' execution was one of the leaders of the young Jerusalem community of Christians and therefore was admirably suited to be presented as the vehicle of special revelations. Finally, there is also an 'Apocalypse of Adam' (NHC V, 5), in which Adam's much younger son Seth (Gen. 4.25) plays a central role, because Adam gives an account to him of the 'knowledge of the eternal God' which had once been taught him by Eve (NHC V, 5, 64, 5–24). The 'knowledge' is brought back by an 'Illuminator' dwelling in a man whose 'flesh is punished' (NHC V, 5, 77, 15f.) and who comes from 'a virgin womb' (78, 20f.). The allusions to the life and destiny of Jesus are clear, even if the name appears only in a very cryptic form and the form of address 'light of the world' (John 8.12) is altered to 'Illuminator'. The title 'Illuminator' was also used in popular philosophy, as is attested by Clement of Alexandria, who quotes a relevant sentence that is also found elsewhere: 'God is an only illuminator of all bringings-forth in heaven and Father of all things.' And Clement concludes: 'These words ... are themselves enough for knowledge of God for him who is able to see only a little way into the truth' (*Admonition* 72, 4f.). By using it, it was again possible to demonstrate the competitiveness of Jewish-Christian teachings to a half-educated public.

Other texts which cannot necessarily be recognized as such by their title can also be classified as apocalypses or more generally as revelation literature. These include the 'Paraphrase of Shem' (NHC VII, 1), which is named after the oldest son of Noah (Gen. 5.32, etc.), in other words after a figure of mythical prehistory who has no sharp profile in the Bible, and who like Seth is made the recipient of revelation. This writing engages in sharp polemic against the idea that 'baptism with the uncleanness of water, that is dark, feeble, idle and destructive, will take away sins' (NHC VII, 1, 37, 22–5). Baptism with water for the forgiveness of sins as practised by the Christian church is regarded as a demonic work. Likewise the people of Sodom, on whom the Old Testament, too, passes an extremely negative verdict, are interpreted as part of the elect race (29, 14f.). The writing, which is difficult to interpret because of considerable philological problems, documents a form of higher 'knowledge' which has already moved a very long way from institutional Christianity – so far, that it rejects the central sacrament of acceptance into the church, baptism, and interprets biblical passages in a sense which is directly opposed to the church's exegesis. This procedure is called 'protest exegesis'. The title 'paraphrase' indicates that here the original revelation to Shem has been abbreviated and elaborated, but the original meaning has been preserved (that at any rate is a contemporary definition, Quintilian, *The Training of the Orator* I, 9, 2). A similar transformation of traditional dogmatics as a protest can also be found in the 'Second Treatise of the Great Seth' (NHC VII, 2; a 'first treatise' has been lost): whereas in the New Testament the apostle Paul interprets baptism as a 'dying with Christ' and calls the Christians 'slaves of God' (Rom. 6.4 and 22), this text engages in polemic against the 'slavery ... that we will die with Christ' (NHC VII, 2, 49, 25–7). Christ, too, 'a fixed notion of a single emanation from the eternal ones' (54, 19f.; 'emanation' is the technical philosophical term for the multiplication of the divine), did not really die:

'It was another [Simon] who bore the cross on his shoulders. It was another upon whom they placed the crown of thorns. But I was rejoicing on high, and I was laughing at their ignorance' (56, 9–19).

Such a notion of a suffering of Christ which was merely apparent and not real is called 'docetism', after the Greek term for 'appear'. It is again to be explained as the assimilation of Christian circles to the religious market of the time: a God who was in principle incapable of suffering had to rest in a state of eternal integrity. If the primitive Christian confession that in Christ 'the fullness of the deity dwelt bodily' (Col. 2.9) was to be maintained, the New Testament accounts of the suffering and death of Jesus caused difficulties. From this perspective it is remarkable that the vast majority of Christian theologians – and moreover also many of those who are assigned to 'gnosis' – opposed such a 'docetic christology' and emphasized the reality of the suffering of Jesus Christ. In the 'Apocalypse of Peter' from the Nag Hammadi Library (NHC VII, 3) there is talk of a bodily part of the Redeemer which is largely assimilated to the church's teaching of two natures of Christ, an earthly one which is capable of suffering and a heavenly one which is not (81, 20). The texts from the find which are strongly focused on non-Christians also include a writing entitled 'Zostrianos' and 'Teachings of Zoroaster' (NHC VIII, 1), which is mentioned by a number of other ancient authors. Thus the adherents of a certain Prodicus, who according to Clement of Alexandria call themselves 'knowers', boast of possessing secret writings of Zoroaster (Clement, *Carpets* I, 69, 6). The Neoplatonic philosopher Porphyry also mentions the text in connection with a description of the Christians in the city of Rome: 'For my part I have compiled numerous refutations of that book named "Zoroaster", pointing out that this is a spurious and new book, forged by the founders of the sect to give the appearance that their teachings derive from the ancient Zoroaster' (Porphyry, *Life of Plotinus* 16). It becomes clear from the content of the passage that at any rate for Porphyry this is a sect ('*haeresis*') *within* Christianity. If we are to trust this information from a third-century philosopher who knew the Christians well and possibly was himself a Christian in his youth (cf. Socrates, *Church History* II, 23, 38 and *Tübinger Theosophie* #85), it is not surprising that there are no explicit references to Christianity in the writing, though there are all kinds of indirect ones. Probably the Neoplatonic philosopher Porphyry did then take up for his own philosophy certain terminological promptings from the writing 'Zostrianos', which he combated so energetically. That is not least the case because in the work itself there are traces of contemporary debates within Platonist philosophy. The writing ends with a sermon by Zostrianos/Zoroaster who summons the 'crowd which has gone astray' to 'awaken their divine part to God'. The Father invites this. As the Greeks already thought that the founder of the Parthian religion, who is surrounded by mythical obscurity, was born 6000 years before Plato (Pliny, *Natural History* XXX, 3), in certain contexts a reference to his revelation could lend special credibility to a new teaching.

In addition, in the Nag Hammadi Library there are prayers like the 'Prayer of Paul' (NHC I, 1) or two prayers for the liturgical eucharist which differ only in tiny details from other contemporary prayers at the eucharist, but stand at the end of a discourse recognizably indebted to the Valentinian system, and which were therefore evidently used among a group of Valentinians (NHC XI, 2A). But all these prayers once again bear witness to the monotheistic structure of the myths, which merely unfold in narrative mode what really belongs together and is also invoked communally in individual or collective prayer: 'Glory be to you through your Son and your offspring Jesus Christ, from now and for ever. Amen' (NHC XI, 2A, 43, 36–8). Moreover the Nag Hammadi find contains hymnic texts like 'The Thunder' ('Bronte', NHC VI, 2), which clearly follows a particular formulary in the discourse of the Egyptian goddess Isis and is also entitled 'The Perfect Mind'.

Finally, the Nag Hammadi find contains clearly non-Christian writings, for example a dialogue between the god Hermes and a disciple, to which the editors give the title 'On the Eighth and the Ninth' (NHC VI, 6), because it depicts the ascent to the eighth and ninth heavenly spheres. This text belongs to a group of ancient writings from Egypt in which the 'Thrice-Great Hermes' interprets the world and life as a revealer against a popular Platonic philosophical background, with occasional references to Egyptian religion and culture. Two further texts of Codex VI also belong to the so-called 'Hermetic literature', namely a prayer (VI, 7) which has also been handed down at another point (Pap. Mimaut col. XVIII, 591–611 and Corpus Hermeticum Asclepius 41b), and a section from the work 'Asclepius' which otherwise has only been preserved in Latin, along with a dialogue (NHC VI, 8). The 'Sentences of Sextus' (NHC XII, 1) contain general rules of wisdom by an otherwise unknown 'Sextus' which have been Christianized in a rather superficial way, and in addition have been preserved in a whole series of languages, dialects and contexts in tradition. 127 sentences are still preserved in the Coptic version from Nag Hammadi: in other versions the collection comprises up to 451 sayings: 'Do not wish to speak first in the midst of a crowd' (Saying 164a; 15, 11–13) or: 'The faithful do not speak many words, but their works are numerous' (Saying 383: 33, 34–6).

The find also contains a not particularly successful translation of a passage from Plato's *Republic* which was extraordinarily popular in antiquity, in which an anthropology is developed with telling images (NHC VI, 5; *Republic* 588A–589B).

The impression has been given, not least by very recent publications, that the Nag Hammadi Library represents the discovery of something like the 'Bible of the Heretics', a rival to the Christian Bible of the church. Beyond doubt the writings, only examples of which could be presented here, contain texts which make a high claim to authority: revelations of Jesus to his disciples are communicated which are not contained in the four canonical Gospels, as are revelations to holy figures of mythical prehistory like Seth, Shem or Zostrianos/Zoroaster.

Although it is impossible to set precise limits to the final literary form of these texts, they certainly do not come from the period before the end of the second century. Now at that time the basic extent of the Christian Bible was already fixed, with some deviations at the periphery. To be able to answer the question whether these writings were really meant as rivals to the canonical scripture of the Christian church we would first of all have to know whether they were read out in worship in place of the Christian Bible or were intended for use only by particularly learned 'knowers' – so to speak as a supplement for the advanced to the canonical Bible. At best we might conjecture from the Sayings Gospels in the find – the Gospel of Thomas and the Gospel of Philip – that these texts were read aloud in worship. In the case of most of the writings found at Nag Hammadi it is much more likely that the biblical books were read and interpreted in their light – 'protest exegesis' is just a particularly extreme example of this. But even then the expression 'Bible of the Heretics' applies to the library only in a very limited sense. We cannot even exclude the possibility that this is a collection made by a pious fourth-century Christian monk in order to know what he thought he had to contest.

The Manichaean discoveries from Turfan

In addition to the discovery of a library of 'gnostic' writings near Nag Hammadi, in the twentieth century further extensive amounts of texts have been discovered which we must presumably likewise interpret as parts of libraries: the Manichaean discoveries from the oasis of Turfan, from Medinet Madi and from the oasis of Dakhleh. In addition there is an individual discovery, the 'Cologne Mani Codex'. In this way many original texts of the Manichaean religion have been brought to light.

The series of such discoveries of Manichaean material began with the four expeditions of the Berlin State Museums between 1902 and 1914 to the Oasis of Turfan, on the Silk Road, which is in the Chinese province of Xinjiang (East Turkestan). Manichaean missionaries had penetrated as far as this region in the eighth century AD. Despite immense difficulties, the Berlin campaigns succeeded in obtaining a rich store of Manichaean texts in West Iranian, Middle Persian, Parthian, East Iranian, Soghdic, Old Turkish (Ugrian) and Chinese. The great linguistic complexity and the wretched state of preservation of the almost 4000 often very tiny fragments have meant that even a century after the beginning of the expeditions the publication of the discoveries has still not been completed, though good progress has been made. Since 1912 the texts have been in the charge of the Akademie der Wissenschaften in Berlin, and there too the work will be completed.

Three extensive sources in Chinese were found in Tunhunang, a western advance post of China in the province of Kan-su, some of which go back to Iranian sources. These texts are now kept in London, Paris and Beijing. They are 'hymn scrolls' ('The last section of Manichaean Hymns'; British Museum Or. 8210, 2659) from the eighth or ninth century, the 'Compendium of Teachings and Rules of Mani, the Buddha of Light' (British Museum, 3969) from the eighth century and the 'Tractate', which presumably dates from the same period, a text which has no original title. All the texts are evidence of the inculturation of Manichaeism in the religious context of Buddhism, as the beginning of the hymn scroll shows (H. 718):

> I reverently laud and praise the tree that blossoms
> eternally,
> Incomparably wonderful, adorned with loud jewels.
> Sustaining all with its trunk, it fills the world;
> Its branches, leaves and fruits are all praiseworthy.
> All the Buddhas come forth from its blossoms,
> and all wisdom arises from its fruits
>
> (H. Schmidt-Glintzer, 11)

The Library of Medinet Madi

The second great Manichaean find of the twentieth century was the Library of Medinet Madi. The Berlin Coptologist Carl Schmidt, who has already been mentioned, was offered papyri on one of his regular stays in Egypt. Schmidt immediately recognized from the headings to pages which bore the working title the 'Chapters of the Master' that these must be fragments of Manichaean doctrinal writings and identified the material as the remains of a Manichaean library. Schmidt succeeded in getting enough money only for part of the papyri, so that they could be acquired by the State Museums in Berlin; another part was purchased by the private collector Alfred Chester Beatty (1875–1968), and these are now in his library in Dublin. Some small pieces found their way into the papyrus collection of the Austrian National Library. Schmidt initiated investigations into the origin of the texts, the language of which seemed to suggest that they came from the neighbourhood of Assiut in Middle Egypt. But they proved to have been found in Medinet Madi, an ancient military colony to the south-west of the Fayum in Lower Egypt. The bad condition of the papyrus books, which as a result of the moistness of the ground had often been fused into lumps, delayed the editing of the approximately 3500 pages, since first the pages had to be detached in laborious and painstaking work, page by page, from the block of the book and put between sheets of glass, while the pages themselves could be read only with a magnifying glass and a mirror. Since Manichaeism is one of the religions of the book, and therefore the Manichaeans had a particular reverence for their sacred books, they used a very fine and extremely thin papyrus; this proved an additional difficulty in the modern conservation of the texts. Schmidt was joined by the Jewish scholar Hans Jakob Polotsky (1905–91), who soon emigrated to Jerusalem; Polotsky first devoted himself to an edition of the 'Manichaean Homilies' and then to editing the 'Chapters of the Teacher'. Charles Robert Cecil Allbery worked on the book of psalms for the Chester Beatty collection. Whereas the Dublin parts of the find survived the Second World War, the Berlin parts were stored in the Soviet Union between the end of the war and 1958, and some of the codices which had not yet been conserved – including letters of Mani – were evidently lost. After editorial work had lain fallow for a long time for various reasons, first of all a facsimile edition was produced on behalf of an international body by the Danish expert Sören Giversen; since then an international team has been working on further editions of the find.

The Medinet Madi collection was evidently part of a Manichaean lay library; at all events it contains few canonical writings of this religious community. The only canonical texts were the book with letters of Mani, who in the information about the sender designates himself 'apostle of Jesus Christ', which unfortunately is largely lost (only parts of it have re-emerged), and a book with 'Collections of the Living Gospel' which contains sections from the 'Living Gospel' or sermons on these sections which were read aloud at assemblies ('*synaxeis*'). Two other volumes in the library served for worship and instruction: the 'Manichaean psalm book' contains a whole series of different collections of hymns made by the Manichaean community. Lectures of Mani and his disciples are contained in the 'Chapters of the Master' (Greek *Kephalaia*), which has already been mentioned, or the 'Chapters of the Wisdom of my Lord Manichaios' (thus

the title of the Dublin parts). Finally, the Medinet Madi
Library also includes a fragmentary codex, which is entitled
'Discourses', 'Logoi'. It contains the so-called 'Manichaean
Homilies', which consist above all of a prayer, the
'Discourse of the Great War' and a report of Mani's passion
and the sufferings of his community after his death.

The Cologne Mani Codex

One of the most exciting single finds of the twentieth
century was a biography of Mani which today is known as
the 'Cologne Mani Codex'. This find from Egypt became
known in 1969, but it is impossible now to discover
precisely where the text comes from. It is a tiny little book
(3.8 × 4.5 cm), which on 192 more or less well preserved
pages contains a collection of excerpts translated from
Syriac into Greek in which in the first third of the fourth
century sections from the works of early Manichaean
authorities were put together into a consecutive biography.
With its many stories, the text reads like a book of pious
entertainment. Moreover, it is so far the only original
Greek text of this community.

The discoveries from the oasis of Dakhleh

In recent years, once again a discovery of Coptic-
Manichaean texts has been made, in Ismant el-Kharab, the
ancient Kellis, in the oasis of Dakhleh. Publication of them
is proceeding apace. The oasis is at about the same latitude
as Nag Hammadi in Upper Egypt, but around 350
kilometres further west, in the middle of the Libyan desert.
The most interesting feature of this investigation is that
here for the first time there are archaeological remains of
a Manichaean community of the early fourth century. At
least one of the houses of this quite remote place was
inhabited by Manichaeans, and a Manichaean community
existed, with some missionary success, contemporaneously
with another Christian community in the same place for
around a century. But evidently there was also a kind of

'Manichaean monastery', though this is attested only by letters and there is as yet no archaeological evidence for it (thus the excavator, Ian Gardner). The texts discovered consist above all of Greek and Coptic letters like Papyrus Kell. Gr. 63, in which 'our Lord, the Paraclete' is mentioned, but also of an account book and Syriac-Coptic lexicons with Manichaean terms (T. Kell, Syr. Kopt. 1). Finally, some parallel texts to the Manichaean psalms which are already known have been found, along with passages from Paul's Letter to the Romans and the Letter to the Hebrews in the New Testament (P. Kell, Copt. 6 and 9). This discovery of texts above all shows something that a careful account of the teaching of this form of religion also indicates (see pp. 101f.). The Manichaeans of this place felt that they were the 'better Christians'.

4. Non-'gnostic' texts

There is of course considerable dispute over the demarcation of this last group of sources; it contains very disparate material from a variety of contexts in the history of ideas. Almost all the texts have already been claimed as witnesses to 'gnosis'. Writings from Graeco-Roman and also Jewish contexts are usually assigned to this group, which contains individual motifs from the list given above. In a survey like this we must content ourselves with characteristic examples.

Hermetic writings

Mention has already been made of the Hermetic writings, to which three texts from the Nag Hammadi Library are assigned. The best-known collection of Hermetic writings, the so-called 'Corpus Hermeticum', goes back to a collection by Byzantine scholars in the tenth century which contains seventeen Greek tractates. We have no information about the authors of these texts and their environment. The tractates, which perhaps come from the third century AD, are regularly termed 'gnostic' because the aim of the Hermetic writings is the knowledge of God. Moreover at least in the first treatise, which is also called 'Poimandres', a myth is told about the origin and destiny of human beings according to which human beings were not made by the supreme God but by a subordinate creator. However, the distinction between a supreme God and the creator is one of the basic assumptions of Platonism at the time of the Roman empire, which is called 'Middle Platonism' – to distinguish it both from the teachings of Plato and from Neoplatonism. Certainly human beings, for whom there is a heavenly model – so to speak a Platonic idea (popularly called 'primordial man', which is open to misunderstanding) – should recognize their heavenly origin. The Greek term 'know' is used in an equally prominent way: 'Holy is God, who wills to be known and is known by his own' (CH I, 31). But in contrast to the texts which are indisputably assigned to 'knowledge', the Hermetic tractate does not feature the forces and powers which seek to keep human beings from knowledge, and therefore there is no redeemer who overcomes them either.

Hekhalot literature

The so-called 'Hekhalot literature' may stand here as an example of Jewish texts. The term is used to denote a corpus of literary tractates from late antiquity which is difficult to date; it has been named after the Hebrew word *hekhalot*, 'halls'. This term denotes the heavenly 'halls' or 'palaces' through which the believer passes to attain the divine throne, located in the seventh sphere of heaven and according to the Old Testament model (Ezek. 1 and 10) portrayed as a chariot. It is called 'Merkabah', so the texts are occasionally also referred to as 'Merkabah mysticism'.

The state of the texts was fluid until the Middle Ages, and they have been constantly revised, so it is difficult to illuminate the process of their growth by literary criticism. A new critical German edition by Peter Schäfer brings together the most important tractates, including 'Hekhalot Rabbati' ('the great palaces'), 'Hekhalot Zutarti' ('the little palaces') and the so-called 'III Enoch'. The Jewish scholar of religion Gershom Scholem has spoken of 'Jewish gnosis' (*Major Trends in Jewish Mysticism*, 1995, 51) because the initiates 'did not want to hand on their secret knowledge, their "gnosis" to everyone', and the knowledge makes it possible for the soul to rise to the highest heaven. However, Scholem already pointed to the differences between the gnostic notions of God and the Merkabah mystics (*Mysticism*, 59). Thus we can probably see points of contact between the ancient movement of 'knowledge' and the 'Hekhalot literature' – say the experience of a completely other-worldly, remote supreme God and the introduction of other divine figures necessitated by this, like that of an angel which is given the solemn Jewish divine name 'little YHWH' (III Enoch #12). But there are also clear differences. Thus for example the mythological drama of a divine element which falls from its sphere into an evil world, slumbers as a divine spark in people of one class and can be freed from this when it is recognized, does not occur. Moreover, by comparison with rabbinic Judaism we must classify such notions more as a subsidiary form of ancient Judaism; accordingly, the Heidelberg New Testament scholar Klaus Berger has called them 'second-hand Judaism'.

III

Early Forms of 'Gnosis' in Antiquity

If we now apply our typological model of 'gnosis' to the sources preserved from antiquity, to literature, inscriptions and other remains, we find a series of persons and writings which in these circumstances may be said to be 'gnostic'. These texts, reports and figures should now be put in chronological order. Here once again it has to be said quite clearly that if the account is based on a typological model it will follow a modern and not an ancient criterion of order. We can distinguish three phases: (a) an early phase, (b) a phase of 'great systems' and (c) the closing phase of Manichaeism as the culmination and end of the development. Because it is still almost impossible to date most texts from the Nag Hammadi Library, these writings will be more tentatively integrated into my reconstruction than the representatives of 'knowledge' in writings of Christian theologians which can be dated well.

If we proceed in this way and investigate ancient sources against the background of our typological model – especially the four groups that I have presented at length – there is no compelling reason for assuming a movement of 'knowledge' corresponding to this model before the change of era or the early first post-Christian century. Simply because of the use of the term, the natural starting point for a history of a movement named 'knowledge' remains that passage from the First Letter to Timothy in the New Testament in which an unknown early Christian theologian under the pseudonym of Paul warns his readers against people who 'wrongly' claim 'knowledge' for themselves (1 Tim. 6.20, cf. p. 5). We saw that while we can speculate about the teachings of this group – presumably these were mythological expansions above all of the biblical narratives about the creation of the world – we cannot make any concrete statements about them. Therefore we can only postulate that at the end of the first or the beginning of the second century (the dating of the letter varies) the first tentative steps were taken to make Christianity competitive in a colourful religious environment by constructing a pre-history and sequel to the biblical history. However, it remains very uncertain whether the opponents contested by the author of the letter already thought along the lines of our typological model that the world and matter were an evil creation, introduced a separate creator God or assistant, and explained the state of the world by a myth of the fall of heavenly beings. Indeed that is improbable. There are no sources for a movement of 'knowledge' corresponding to our typological model in the first century. Only in the second century do we have corresponding accounts, and they also fit the changed historical situation of Christianity, which now had to prove itself in the ancient metropolitan centres of education in the competition between the religions and philosophies.

The late dating of 'knowledge' argued for here has been put in question time and again. At the end of the nineteenth century Moriz Friedländer postulated that there had been a Jewish 'gnosis' as early as the first century BC (*Das vorchristliche jüdische Gnosticismus*, Göttingen 1898). And time and again passages of the literature of ancient Judaism have been regarded as 'gnostic'; texts from the Nag Hammadi find have been claimed as evidence for a purely Jewish 'gnosis' (for example the 'Apocalypse of Adam', NHC V, 5), or at least a Jewish 'gnosis' has been postulated as a presupposition for Christian 'gnosis'.

Closely connected with such hypotheses was the question whether the writings which found their way into the canon of the New Testament in the second century would not amount to witnesses to a 'gnosis' at the root of Christianity. We must investigate these two complexes briefly before continuing our history of the development of 'knowledge'.

1. Jewish 'gnosis'?

The question of a Jewish 'gnosis' arises simply because time and again notions or elements occur in the texts which are usually assigned to 'gnosis' which can be observed in many texts of ancient Jewish literature. As we saw, in the corpus of the 'Hekhalot literature' (see above, p. 64) an angel standing particularly close to the divine throne is called 'little Yahweh' (III Enoch #12 [Schäfer, Synopse #15, line 8]). And the first writing in the Codex Askewianis, the so-called 'Pistis Sophia' (see above, p. 40), knows a good divine power which manifests itself in John the Baptist and is called the 'little Jao' (p. 7, 36; 8, 11). Despite all the differences between the two notions we cannot avoid assuming a certain influence – perhaps through intermediaries. Reference has also been made time and again to Judaism for the depictions of the heavenly court, of visions and heavenly journeys of the kind that appear in the Nag Hammadi writings; for the names of angels and demons; for the notion of the hermaphroditic nature of the first human being, and many other details. The central role of a divine partial sphere by the name of 'Wisdom', the aeon of Sophia, in many systems would be inconceivable without the Jewish wisdom literature: here too Wisdom could be thought of as an independent divine figure, to such a degree that she could even be described in the image of a child playing before God (cf. Prov. 8.30). Finally, mention could also be made of the magical words which appear in a variety of Coptic texts. Thus in the first book of the same name from the Codex Brucianus the divine figure Jeû is also called 'ioeiaothouicholmio' (p. 261, 1 and 5); such secret names, which at the same time attest that the divine cannot be named with earthly names, were regularly formed from variants of the Jewish name of God and from Jewish names for angels. However, in the rabbinic literature of ancient Judaism, time and again there was polemic against the notion of 'two forces in heaven', in other words against the assumption of a creator turned away from the supreme God, and the talk of a male-female primordial human being was discussed critically. So we cannot exclude the possibility that in the period of the Roman empire there were individual Jewish scholars who advocated these views. However, there is no text in extant ancient Jewish literature which contains the various motifs which according to our model characterize the ancient movement of 'knowledge' as completely and clearly as, say, the texts from Nag Hammadi or Medinet Madi. The writings found in these libraries cannot be used as an argument for an origin of 'gnosis' in Judaism either: they are interested in the Old Testament only to the degree that it contains a history of creation up to the story of the flood, which is interpreted. Time and again words from the Jewish Bible are also put in the mouth of the creator God: 'I am a jealous God and beside me there is no God' (Ex. 20.5 and Isa. 45.5: HA, NHC II, 4, 86, 30f.; 94, 22f., etc.). As we saw, the 'Teachings of Silvanus' (NHC VII, 4) from Nag Hammadi engage in polemic against this notion: 'Let no one ever say that God is ignorant. For it is not right to put the Creator of every creature – here the original has the Greek loanword *demiourgos* – in ignorance' (p. 116, 5–9). But no independent interest in other biblical books, for example the legal texts, which one might expect of pious Jews, can be demonstrated either in the Nag Hammadi writings or in those of Medinet Madi. Therefore it probably makes more sense to speak of Jewish roots of 'gnosis' rather than of a fully developed 'Jewish gnosis'. Likewise we do not find any self-designation 'Knower' in the sources of ancient Judaism either.

The question whether 'gnosis' can also be observed at the roots of Christianity in the first extant written texts is

just as vigorously disputed as the thesis that there was a
'Jewish gnosis' as the presupposition for a Christian
'gnosis'.

2. 'Gnosis' in the New Testament?

The Gospel of John

In research, a 'gnostic' character has always been claimed
above all for two complexes of writings which were
canonized in the second century as part of the 'New
Testament', namely the Gospel of John and certain letters
from the school of the apostle Paul. In particular, in the
twentieth century it was thought that the first signs of
the Christianizing of an originally pagan gnosis could be
observed in this Gospel, but first sources had to be
postulated for it. Above all the distinguished Marburg
New Testament scholar Rudolf Bultmann (1884–1976)
attempted to show with an impressive commentary on the
Gospel of John that central views of the Gospel were 'part
of a gnostic doctrine of redemption' which had been trans-
ferred to the person of Jesus and regarded the author as a
Christianized gnostic (*Glauben und Verstehen* IV, [4]1984, 145).
However, at decisive points the basic outlines of the Gospel
of John do not fit the typological model outlined above:
according to the Gospel, which follows Jewish-Hellenistic
ideas here, the creation goes back to the Word of God
(Greek 'Logos'; cf. John 1.1–4), which already exists before
the world, and not to a creator who is opposed to God. For
the author of the Gospel of John it is evident, particularly
in Jesus' suffering on the cross, that Jesus Christ is the one
Word of God, which has assumed a human body.
Such an emphasis on the identity between the body of
the earthly Jesus and the reality of a heavenly redeemer
differs markedly from the occasionally more energetic,
occasionally more cautious differentiations of the literature
of Nag Hammadi and Medinet Madi. Certainly, as I have
already mentioned (p. 33), the first extant ancient
commentary on the Gospel of John comes from Heracleon,

an adherent of the school of the Roman teacher
Valentinus, and many outlines of systems which with
good reason can be assigned to 'knowledge' use terms
and notions from the Fourth Gospel. But this striking
preference could also simply be connected with the fact
that the Gospel of John is the only one of the four
canonical Gospels to begin with the creation of the world
and thus is particularly attractive as a biblical basis for
theologians who are interested in total theories. The same
goes for abrupt separations between light and darkness or
between God and the world with which the Gospel offered
additional points of contact.

Ephesians and Colossians

Some have also wanted to see reflections of a 'gnostic'
system in these two letters, which come from circles of
disciples of the apostle Paul but were handed down under
his name, that is, the primordial man myth that has already
been mentioned. The author of the Letter to the Ephesians
is said to have provided a variation on this notion with his
talk of a 'new being' (Eph. 2.15) and 'perfect man' (Eph.
4.13). Above all the notion of the church as the 'body of
Christ' expressed in the two letters has been regarded as
gnostic (Heinrich Schlier, *Christus und Kirche im Epheserbrief,*
1930, 27–48). Now it has proved possible not only to
demonstrate that there never was a primordial man myth in
the sense presupposed, but that the notions of the so-called
'deutero-Pauline letters' can also be derived quite easily
from contemporary Judaism. In any case there is no
mention in these letters of a defective creation and creator
or angelic powers which are opposed to God, and nowhere
is there any hint of a differentiation between the historical
Jesus and a heavenly Christ-figure. In view of this evidence,
it is also utterly improbable that Paul himself or these
letters are already arguing against developed mythological
systems. That had time and again been claimed, for
example, for Paul's First Letter to the Corinthians or
for Colossians, which warns against being trapped by

'philosophy and empty deceit' (Col. 2.8). Meanwhile it has become clearer that of course the Christian communities to which the letters collected in the New Testament are addressed shared the ideas and notions of their religious environment: they were interested in 'knowledge'; they wanted to understand their Christianity against the background of contemporary philosophical offers of meaning and were open to religious practices and speculations in the borderlands between the religions. At all events, this literature too leads to the prehistory of the movement that I want to go on to describe.

3. Early representatives of 'gnosis'

Simon Magus

Irenaeus of Lyons asserts in his *Refutation*, which has already been mentioned, that 'the "knowledge" falsely so-called' began with the magician Simon from Samaria, who is already mentioned in the Acts of the Apostles, and was also advocated by his followers, whom he calls 'Simonians' (*Refutation* I, 23, 4). Now a surprising feature in this ancient reconstruction of 'knowledge' is that according to the testimony of the Acts of the Apostles Simon was a magician, and nothing is reported of any doctrinal system of this magician. According to the New Testament report his sole interest was to exercise power over reality. He is said to have been converted to Christianity because the adherents of the new movement who were engaged in a mission in Samaria could deal powerfully with the sick and heal them (Acts 8.9–19). The Acts of the Apostles also reports that Simon gained a following as a successful magician and was called 'Great Power of God' on account of his capacities (Acts 8.10).

Just a century after the events depicted in the Acts of the Apostles, around the middle of the second century, the Christian theologian Justin, who was active in Rome, attests in his First Apology that the magician Simon has a community of adherents in the capital, mainly consisting of

Samaritans. Since his visit to Rome these have been worshipping him as a god. In this connection Justin mentions a statue on the island on the Tiber in Rome and reports its inscription: 'to the holy god Simon'. In 1574 the statue and the inscription were discovered, and since then it has been known that in rendering the text Justin went wrong over a single but decisive letter: the statue was not dedicated to the magician Simon but to Semo Sancus, the ancient Roman god of oaths, who was also called 'holy god' (CIL VI, 567). For want of any other evidence, whether the 'Simonians' of Rome in fact worshipped Simon at the Semo statue or Christians only believed this must remain an open question. At any rate Semo was connected with the supreme god Jupiter, so that it is at least probable that the 'Simonians', who indeed evidently regarded Simon as a 'representative' of the supreme God, also identified him with a 'representative' of the supreme God of the Romans. Such identifications of gods were quite customary at the time of the empire. Likewise Irenaeus reports that the 'Simonians' worshipped an image of Simon which imitated the form of Jupiter (*Refutation* I, 23, 4). Justin's report that the 'Simonians' worshipped not only Simon as the first god but a former prostitute by the name of Helen who travelled with him as the first idea, and thus as a partial authority of this first god (*Refutation* I, 26, 2f.), is even more interesting. For Helen fits the report in Irenaeus, just 30 years later, that a system was widespread among the 'Simonians' in which the idea of the first god created angels and powers which in turn had created this world. In Irenaeus, too, Simon is identified as a representative of the supreme God and the former prostitute Helen as the representative of a divine partial authority, the first idea (*Refutation* I, 23, 2f.). In this system the angels are depicted as evil; they know nothing of the supreme god, seize the first idea, i.e. a partial sphere of God, and imprison it in earthly matter. The supreme god therefore came in the form of Simon himself in order to redeem from matter the divine part represented by Helen. Thus not only is Simon, like Jesus, worshipped by his followers as a god; a kind of counter-scheme to the Christian doctrine of redemption, a kind of 'counter-christology', is narrated.

Now in contrast to the New Testament writings discussed earlier, this system, the beginnings of which Irenaeus reports, not without polemic, contains the most important elements of our typological model for 'gnosis'. There are creators (namely the angels) who are very clearly separated from the supreme god and have negative connotations. Their creation is likewise viewed in a negative way: Helen's brothel is a telling symbol for the depth to which partial aspects of God can fall in this creation. Irenaeus says that belief in Simon and Helen is enough for people to be saved (*Refutation* I, 23, 3).

Two decisive questions about Simon and the 'Simonians' remain. How old is this system, which is clearly 'gnostic' in the sense of our model? And: is it a Christian system? If the author of the New Testament Acts of the Apostles is not concealing anything important (and we have no occasion to assume this), then the 'Simonian system' came into being only after the death of Simon, who was merely a magician, and also only after the New Testament book was written. Thus at the earliest it can come from the first decades of the second century, though the first certain evidence of the whole mythological narrative is Irenaeus at the end of the century. Irenaeus presents the system in his introduction as a Christian system, because he reports as the teaching of Simon that 'he it was who appeared among the Jews as Son, but in Samaria descended as Father and came to the other peoples as Holy Spirit' (*Refutation* I, 23, 1). This would be clear competition with the Christian notion of the one God in his three modes of existence, Father, Son and Holy Spirit, a competition which would fit the historical note in the Acts of the Apostles that Simon was initially close to the Christian community and that there was a division later. Other reports about Simon's stay in Rome also fit this. Therefore this system of 'knowledge' would be an attempt by Simon's followers to oppose their own teaching to the Christian theology taking shape in Rome. That it was intended for Christians can be recognized from the fact that according to Irenaeus' report the 'Simonians' interpreted the well-known New Testament parable of the lost sheep (Matt. 18.12f.//Luke 15.4–6) against the background of their thesis of the divine element imprisoned in the world and as a statement about Helen (*Refutation* I, 23, 2). Likewise, the system is also aimed at winning over non-Christians: Irenaeus reports that Helen, Simon's companion, was identified with the Helen of the Trojan War. If, moreover, we read the account of the system through the eyes of a contemporary with a philosophical education, we discover hidden analogies to the popular Platonic notion of a divine world soul, parts of which are imprisoned in human bodies and which must wander through human beings from generation to generation until it is freed from the prison of the body (*Timaeus* 41D–42D). A hidden reference to popular Platonic notions is also recognizable in the report that the 'Simonians' had worshipped a statue of Athena as Helen. As the idea which had sprung from the head of Zeus, Athena represented the heavenly models of earthly reality, the ideas (Varro in Augustine, *City of God* VII, 28). The mythological narrative of the wandering Helen, who is indeed merely the linguistic garb for a fundamentally timeless development of the divine, will have reminded Jews of their traditions about the heavenly Wisdom which wandered unrecognized and scorned among human beings (Sir. 24.1–8; Wisd. 7.27). Moreover the symbolic marriage of a prostitute (if this is not later polemic against Helen) already has a model in the Old Testament. On the command of his God, the prophet Hosea married such a woman (Hos. 1.2f.). Furthermore the 'Exegesis on the Soul' explicitly quotes the Old Testament verses (NHC II, 6, 129, 23–130, 10). However, we can hardly establish with any certainty to what extent specific elements which distinguished the belief of the Samaritans from the Judaism that was closely related to it were also integrated into the system of the 'Simonians'.

So is 'gnosis' to be understood as a non-Christian competitor to the Christian theology which was gradually developing in the second century? The other names which

Irenaeus mentions in his account of the beginnings of
'gnosis', and above all the systems that he attributes to
these names, necessarily raise considerable doubts about
such a thesis.

Menander

The next early representative of 'knowledge' after Simon
whom Irenaeus mentions is a Menander, who likewise
comes from Samaria. Justin, too, mentions him just 30 years
previously as a disciple of Simon, but knows only that he
was a magician who was also active in Antioch in Syria.
Irenaeus attributes to him a variant of the system of the
'Simonians', namely the doctrine that the first power
is unknown. Only the Redeemer can be known, and is
identical with that Menander – and not with Simon.
Through magical arts one can attain the 'knowledge' with
which one even has the 'power of the angels which created
the world' (*Refutation* I, 23, 5). Whereas Justin reports that
Menander only made his followers believe that they would
not die, according to Irenaeus a baptism in Menander is
said to have this effect. If we are to take this last report at all
seriously, then like the rest of the system it is again to be
understood merely as competing with Christian theology.
Whereas Christian baptism preserves people from final
death only in the last judgement on the Last Day,
Menander's baptism already rescues them from earthly
death. Evidently it was claimed that with the redeemer
Menander the messianic age had already dawned in which
the members of the community of salvation would no
longer grow old (Book of Jubilees 23.28).

Saturninus

The next early representative of 'gnosis' to be mentioned
by Irenaeus is a Saturninus (often also in the Greek form of
this name, Satornilus), from Antioch in Syria. Irenaeus
attributes to him a variant of the system put forward by
Menander: the first God, here called Father, is unknown to

all. The world was made by seven angels, and human beings, too, are a creation of the angels, whereas the angels are a creation of the unknown supreme God. Man is created after an image which was shown briefly by the absolute power, but so defectively that he 'had to creep like a worm' (*Refutation* I, 24, 1). Then out of compassion the supreme God sent a spark of life 'which raised man up, established him and gave him life'. In Saturninus' system, too, there is a saviour called 'Christ': he appeared only as the semblance of man, brings salvation to the good and overthrows the angelic powers which are hostile to God. Finally, Irenaeus reports another detail in the lifestyle of the followers of Saturninus: they renounced marriage, children and food containing meat. The relationship of this system to Menander claimed by Irenaeus seems contrived, especially as we know only from Justin that the two worked in Antioch in Syria. Rather – if we may trust the source – Saturninus developed an independent system in which the supreme God is relieved of the craft of creation by seven angels: presumably an angel was responsible for each day of the week of creation. As we saw, the notion of creation by angels is indebted to the popular Platonic notion that the supreme God might not be entrusted with crafts like making a human being. The idea that nevertheless the supreme God was involved in creation by means of a 'spark of life' is not original either: the Jewish-Hellenistic thinker Philo of Alexandria used a similar metaphor to safeguard the relationship between God and his image (*The Legacy of the Divine* 309). The view that Christ became only the semblance of man is intended as it were to preserve a clear philosophical division between God and human beings. The emphasis on an ascetic way of life likewise links the group with specific trends in popular philosophy. Strikingly, Saturninus' system has a crude anti-Jewish emphasis, since it is reported without any explanation that 'the God of the Jews' – in the view of most Christians the Father of Jesus Christ – is, like Satan, one of the angels created by the supreme God. In contrast to the systems which Irenaeus attributes to the followers of Simon and his pupil Menander, this is clearly a Christian system, since a Christ-figure plays a central role. Several ancient authors date Saturninus to the time of the emperor Hadrian (AD 117–38; e.g. Eusebius, *Church History* IV, 7, 3). We do not know whether or not the system arose at this time. However, beyond doubt it must be regarded as 'gnosis' in the sense of our typological model.

Basilides

The Christian teacher Basilides, who was active in Alexandria, is the first among the early representatives of 'gnosis' in Irenaeus of whom a few authentic fragments of text have been preserved, along with original texts from his school. However, the position that we can recognize from these texts differs considerably from what Irenaeus reports about Basilides. This clearly indicates a considerable problem in the reconstruction of the early history of 'gnosis': over wide areas we cannot check the reports of Justin and Irenaeus by other texts, but must reckon with crude errors and distortions. It emerges from the fragments that in all probability Basilides published under the title 'Expositions' his own version of the Gospel of Luke with a relatively free commentary in 24 volumes. This publication itself shows that he taught Christianity like one of the numerous scholars with a philological orientation in the cultural metropolis of Alexandria. So Basilides is evidence that only about a century after the death of Jesus, Christianity was interesting to a particular form of higher learning. If we may take the few fragments of Basilides with those that are attributed to a son named Isidore and his school, the following picture of his system emerges. Like Saturninus, Basilides distinguished between the supreme God and the god of this world (Fragments 4 and 14). By analogy, he made a distinction between the real human soul and its bad 'attachments', the passions, which ultimately come from primal matter. Moreover, he advocated the Platonic doctrine of the migration of souls (Fragments 17 and 18). Thus while they adopted

contemporary Platonic theories about the soul very freely,
Basilides and his son did not want to take part in the philosophical debate about the soul, but to reply to specific
pastoral questions about human action in such a way that
semi-educated contemporaries were not deterred by the
level of their answer. The pastoral interest of this
theory becomes clear from Basilides' explanation that the
suffering which Christians have to endure for their faith is
God's punishment for possibly hidden sins (Fragment 7).
The doctrine of the migration of souls is also primarily
intended to reassure anxious Christians that there is a
correspondence between moral status and individual
destiny, which merits addressing God as just: moral
behaviour is rewarded with good life. At this point an early
Christian theology was only going by what the educated
world of its time was saying, and that is really not surprising.
But its Christian stamp is also evident from the way in
which the proclamation of the gospel – initially an event
which took place on earth at a particular place at a
particular time – is raised to the divine level by Basilides:
the gospel is also proclaimed to the god of this world, and
initially he becomes fearful, but then hopeful (Fragment
4). So here a Christian thinker is making an effort to
hand on the fundamental facts of the Christian history of
salvation on the basis of a Platonizing picture of the world.
The teaching of the Basilidians is therefore to be distinguished from 'gnosis' in the sense of our typological model
because Basilides made it the task of all men and women 'to
stand in love to all things, because each thing preserves a
relationship to the All' (Fragment 8 = Clement, *Carpets* IV,
86, 1). In this system the world is not regarded as an evil
creation. However, the system is on the way towards
becoming a 'gnosis' because various divine figures are
separated. Still, the lower God is not fundamentally evil,
but co-operates with the supreme God in redemption.

Irenaeus' report about Basilides sounds quite different:
according to it the Father, who is himself unbegotten, first
of all sets in motion the procreation of five partial aspects
of himself: mind, word, thought, wisdom and power. But

other divine forces with a lower status have arisen from the combination of wisdom and power, until all in all 365 heavens full of such beings have been completed, matching the number of the days of the year (*Refutation* I, 24, 3). The ruler of the last heaven is the 'God of the Jews', who is opposed by the other rulers. They have created the world and evidently also human beings. In this situation the supreme God has 'sent his mind, which is called Christ, to free those who believe in him from the power of those who have made the world' (*Refutation* I, 24, 4). A 'docetic christ-ology' (see above, p. 55) is followed: Simon of Cyrene was crucified in the place of Jesus Christ; he acted for Jesus, while Jesus stood by and laughed. Anyone who has knowledge of these circumstances is no longer under the authority of the ruler angels who created the world. It is evident how little this system, which Irenaeus attributes to Basilides, fits his extant fragments. We can even still recognize that Irenaeus has evidently never read a line of Basilides, since he accuses the Basilidians of avoiding martyrdom by denying their Christianity under the slogan 'Know all, but none shall know you.' But that hardly matches Basilides' pastoral advice to people who are asking why they have to suffer martyrdom.

The state of the tradition is further complicated by the fact that at the beginning of the third century Hippolytus, too, reports a system of the Basilidians which differs markedly from that reported by Irenaeus (*Refutation* VII, 20–27). Whatever one thinks about the question whether it fits the extant fragments or is not better understood as a very late system from the school of Basilides – here too the earthly world is no more thought of as being fundamentally evil than is its ruler, and that at any rate admirably fits the picture one gets of these fragments.

The beginnings of 'gnosis' – a summary

The previous section on Basilides makes it clear how any reconstruction of the beginnings of 'gnosis' rests on very thin ice. If we begin from the safest component in the

uncertain foundation of the sources – the tradition in
Basilides – it becomes clear that Justin and Irenaeus, our
main informants, had only very general information, which
they filled out in accordance with a scheme. This need not
have been malice on the part of these authors, but simply
the consequence of a lack of information. This evidence
could become even clearer if we treated with equal
thoroughness the reports on the other representatives of
'gnosis' covered by Irenaeus, the sections on Carpocrates
(*Refutation* I, 25, 1–5), Cerinthus (26,1), the Barbelo-
gnostics (29,1–4), the 'snake people' (Ophites) and the
'Seth people' (Sethians) (30, 1–14). The scheme which
Irenaeus used as a basis for all these early representatives
and which to this degree gives his normal model for early
'gnosis', consisted of the following points:

- According to Irenaeus, all the early representatives
  mentioned teach the creation of the world by lower
  angels and the consequent defectiveness of creation.
  Redemption is synonymous with knowledge of this
  state.

- All the representatives identify the redeemer with a
  partial aspect of the supreme God or a power
  deriving from him, but see the connection between
  this redeemer figure and the earthly Jesus as a
  problem.

- Almost all representatives identify the God attested
  in the Jewish Bible with a subordinate or even fallen
  partial aspect of the supreme God.

We can demonstrate from both the reports about Simon
and the fragments of Basilides that the systems which
Irenaeus describes with a clear reference to his normal
system represent at least secondary stages of theoretical
development. Neither Simon in the first century nor
Basilides in the early second century taught what Irenaeus
asserted at the end of the second century. That also arouses
the suspicion that Irenaeus has constructed from other
sources the system he sees as a rival to Christianity and

attributes to Simon, in order to have at the beginning of the development an anti-Christian scheme by the first 'heretic' to be mentioned in the Bible which is as pagan as possible. It would follow from this that a modern reconstruction of 'gnosis' should not begin with Simon the magician.

In that case, can the early history of 'gnosis' then be reconstructed at all? At all events we can indicate some corner-stones of the development which emerge from a careful analysis of the sources. 'Gnosis' evidently came into being – as the traditions about Basilides show – in the metropolitan centres of education in antiquity, as an attempt by semi-educated people to explain their Christianity at the level of the time. In the process, elements that Jewish-Hellenistic thinkers had already used were taken over from popular philosophy: a strict division was made between the supreme God and the divine forces involved in creation, and this distinction was also applied to the figure of Christ. The Christian usage differed from the Jewish-Hellenistic usage in that the 'God of the Jews' was not identified, as in Philo of Alexandria, with the supreme God, but put at the level of the subordinate divine powers. The sudden emergence of a marked 'darkening' of the view of the world in the outlines of these systems, for which there are virtually no contemporary parallels, is difficult to explain: both creation generally and human beings in particular are felt to be damaged. This world-view separates not only those systems from Jewish-Hellenistic schemes, but also for example the fragments of Basilides from the system that Irenaeus and Hippolytus attribute to him. This is possibly the way in which Christian thinkers coped with the fact that after the death of Jesus the promised end of the world had not come, and that while his community grew, it did so only slowly, and was exposed to harsh persecutions. If more than 90 per cent of all people rejected Christianity, humankind and the world could not be a creation of the supreme God.

IV

The Great Systems of Ancient 'Gnosis'

If we investigate the 'great systems' of the late second and early third centuries, for which there is substantially better evidence, the picture that we obtained in the analysis of reports about early representatives of 'gnosis', many features of which were uncertain, is confirmed.

The circles of those who handed it on consist essentially of groups of more or less well-educated Christians who gathered around charismatic teachers in analogy to the established philosophical schools or free circles of hearers. Here Christian theology was expounded before the forum of semi-educated city-dwellers and developed in accordance with the standards of the time: anyone after Plato who wanted to speak about God, the world, the soul and the destiny of human beings had to do so in the form of a myth, because there was no other form of God, the world and the soul in the world of earthly experience which could be depicted in language (Plato, *Letter* 7, 344D, and *Timaeus* 28C). 'Therefore the friend of myth is in a sense also a philosopher,' we read in Aristotle (*Metaphysics* I, 2, 982b 18). Philosophical myths, as distinct from age-old popular myths, were a deliberate artistic creation. Therefore the principles of their construction have to be noted when we interpret them: thus developments within the one deity which have neither location nor duration are unfolded by the narrative in space and time. So those who, like the

Christian critics of 'gnosis', mock the 'swarm' of divine partial authorities in myth and thus approximate Christian 'gnosis' to polytheism have not understood that here a very careful distinction between partial aspects of the deity was being narrated in the form of a history of the development of God. Moreover, in these Christian schools of 'knowledge', as well as myth there was also the attempt to develop what was meant at the level of philosophical dialogue, in the form of lectures, scholarly commentaries on the text, or extended tractates. Unfortunately only fragments of such texts have been preserved, because evidently the colourful myths fascinated people more than the dry discourses on them.

Here I shall introduce above all the Marcionites, the Valentinians and the so-called Barbelo-gnostics as an example of great 'gnostic' schools.

1. Marcion and the Marcionites

Marcion came from Sinope and was a ship-owner (or export trader: Tertullian, *Indictment against the Heretics* 30, 1; *Against Marcion* I, 18, 4). He belongs only very indirectly in a history of 'gnosis', because he was basically a Christian thinker with a quite individual stamp. But I shall discuss him here on the one hand because by a doctrine of two gods which he advocated he forced other 'gnostics' to expound more clearly their position on whether there was only one single God. On the other hand his system is related at least at some points to the others discussed here.

Around the year AD 140 he joined the Christian community in Rome and contributed a not inconsiderable sum of money to the common purse. Just four years later the community expelled him because of his theology and returned the sum that he had donated. Thereupon Marcion began on an intensive missionary activity which was evidently very successful: in the middle of the flat countryside just twenty kilometres south of Damascus an inscription has been found which mentions a 'synagogue of the Marcionites of the village of Lebaba of the Lord and Saviour Jesus Christ' and goes on to report that this building was constructed in AD 318/19 'under the direction of the presbyter Paul' (Le Bas/Waddington III, 1, no. 2558), and at the beginning of the fifth century a bishop from North Syria could still write that he had cured eight villages in his diocese of Marcionitism (Theodoret of Cyrrhus, *Letter* 81).

Although no lengthy texts of Marcion's have been preserved, we can make a critical reconstruction of his system indirectly from the polemic above all in Tertullian. Like Basilides, he was first of all a philologist of the biblical texts who, in accordance with the scholarly practice of his time and of today, produced critical editions of texts and wrote commentaries on them. Marcion edited the particular writings which found their way into a canonical New Testament on the basis of a radical reading of the letters of the apostle Paul and – like the representatives of early 'gnosis' before him – made a distinction between the supreme, 'alien' God and the creator God attested in the Old Testament, who bears the old Platonic title 'craftsman' (*demiourgos*; cf. *Timaeus* 41A and *Republic* 530A). In philosophy at the time of the Roman empire the word was predominantly used for the supreme God, but there were exceptions, like the contemporary Platonic philosopher Numenius from Apamea in Syria, who, like Marcion and representatives of 'gnosis', separated a supreme God and Father from the creator god called 'demiurge'. But evidently one factor in Marcion's own development of this position was that, like philologists of a particular school, he took certain statements in the Bible in an uncompromising literal sense, e.g. a statement in Isaiah 45.7: 'I create evil' (cf. Tertullian, *Against Marcion* I, 2, 2). Marcion understood the Jewish Bible, for which the expression 'Old Testament' emerged at the end of the second century, and which had hitherto unquestioningly been presupposed in Christianity as canonical holy scripture, as an expression of the 'demiurge' and therefore felt entitled in his review of the Christian Bible to remove passages which referred to it as falsifications. In a separate exegetical companion to his edition of the Bible, the (lost) 'Antitheses', Marcion contrasted statements from the two Testaments in a sharp radicalization of the Pauline antithesis of law and gospel. Paul, too, had indeed already contrasted law and gospel as two ways to salvation, but he had never claimed two different gods as originators or even defamed the whole of the Jewish Bible as an exclusive testimony to the law. However, on the basis of a strict concept of God in which the philosophical predicate of immutability evidently played a major role, Marcion could not present one and the same God as author of two modes of salvation, and he also foisted this position on Paul. According to Marcion, one could not read anything about the good, alien God in the Old Testament; rather, out of his sheer goodness the alien God suddenly revealed himself through his Christ – this motif also appears in Basilides (Tertullian, *Against Marcion* III, 20, 2f.). Of course, in this system no really close connection between this good God and the earthly world is conceivable: therefore Jesus Christ appears in this world in a disembodied form and is not even born. But evidently he dies a quite real death on the cross to ransom human beings from the curse of the law. Here Marcion was simply repeating basic elements of Pauline theology. Anyone who has accepted the revelations of the good and alien God must turn away completely from the evil creation: Marcion therefore required strict asceticism of his followers (Tertullian, *Against Marcion* I, 29, 2 and 5).

Two points distinguish Marcion radically from the teachers of the second and third century whom we can assign to 'gnosis' on the basis of our typological model. First of all, his system lacks any mythological narrative about a differentiation in the concept of God into 'eternities' (aeons) or comparable analogies to the Platonic notional figure of the ideas. Nor is the figure of Jesus Christ split or his real death put in doubt. Secondly, Marcion emphasizes – here fully in accord with the apostle Paul – that only the goodness of God has redeemed all human beings from their radical corruption. We read nothing in

Marcion of a 'divine spark of light' in human beings or in a particular group of human beings, as with Saturninus.

2. Valentinus and the Valentinians

Valentinus was a respected Christian teacher who, like Justin, taught in Rome around the middle of the second century, and was even proposed by his Christian community as a candidate for higher office in the community. If Irenaeus' information is correct, Valentinus came to Rome before 140 and worked there for at least fifteen years without being attacked (*Refutation* III, 4, 3). Born in Egypt and probably educated in Alexandria, for unknown reasons he went to Cyprus in the 160s (Epiphanius, *Medicine Chest* II, 31, 2, 1f. and 7, 1f.). Thus he could no longer defend himself against the views which Christian teachers disseminated in his name and under the aegis of a respected theologian of the city of Rome. As in the case of Basilides, only a very few fragments of his work have been preserved: above all fragments of letters, sermons and a hymn, which show that this Christian teacher was a gifted poet. If we may believe the fragments, like many other early representatives of 'gnosis' Valentinus thought that human beings were made imperfectly by angels but perfected in the act of creation by the supreme God in accordance with a heavenly model (Fragments 1 and 5). He is quite different from thinkers like Saturninus and others, because in his hymns – like Basilides – he regards the whole world as a well-ordered creation permeated by the spirit of God (Fragment 8). As with many other Christian theologians of the time, a strictly ascetic note pervades this theology: the revelation of the highest God, the 'only good Father', which takes place through his son Jesus Christ, purifies the corrupt human heart, which like a bad tourist hotel is filled with all sorts of refuse and rubbish (Fragment 2). No distinction is evidently made between Jesus and Christ; the earthly Jesus of Nazareth proves his divine being by eating and drinking but not excreting, because as God he really needs no nourishment and so has no digestive processes (Fragment 3). This teaching, which is quite remarkable in its details, only shows that Valentinus, like Basilides, belongs so to speak to an experimental phase of Christian theology which as yet had relatively few standards. People were still seeking how to explain particular Christian standpoints – for example that the man Jesus was a God – to their semi-educated contemporaries. Like Basilides, Valentinus, too, is a thinker who prepares the way for the great systems of 'gnosis', but does not take it himself. However, such differences between teachers and those who actually were or claimed to be their pupils were nothing special in antiquity; rather, they showed the originality and goodness of a philosophical school.

Justin already knows in the middle of the second century a school of Christian thinkers who saw themselves as being in the tradition of Valentinus; the name 'Valentinians' which they took followed the practice of calling members of philosophical schools after their founders, for example 'Platonists', even if they did not put forward the teachings of Plato in the specific sense. At the beginning of his *Refutation*, 30 years after Justin, Irenaeus of Lyons cites a great mythological system of 'Valentinian gnosis' which a later marginal note has attributed to a teacher by the name of Ptolemy who likewise lived in Rome (*Refutation* I, 1,1–8, 5). In essence this 'great system' consists of a prehistory and a sequel to the biblical narratives about creation and redemption which presuppose the contemporary Platonic theory of principles and neo-Pythagorean number speculation. In the Valentinian system the supreme God is called 'Bythos', the Greek term for 'abyss' or 'depth', as in the 'deeps of the sea'. Thus the term already signals that the supreme God is unfathomable and has become accessible only through the revelation of his Son. This image of God not only corresponds to particular New Testament writings, but is also the common view of many ancient philosophies. In accordance with the model of the Platonic doctrine of ideas, divine partial aspects, eternities ('aeons'), proceed from this God, who is utterly other-worldly and unknowable – at this point the Valentinians use the technical philosophical vocabulary which Plotinus, too, will use in the third century to describe the process of the unfolding of the One. However, as with most of the Christian theologians of antiquity, the Platonic technical term 'idea' is carefully avoided, in order to emphasize the originality of the system. The names of these divine partial aspects are taken above all from the Gospel of John and the doctrine of God in contemporary popular philosophy, and to a degree are a somewhat random enumeration of classical properties of God. That all 'eternities' together are called divine 'fullness' and their number stands symbolically for the innumerable fullness of the divine glories makes it clear that here we do not have many gods but partial aspects of a single God. An ideal model is constructed on the divine level for the fall of the first human couple, namely the fall of the divine eternity 'Wisdom'. It ultimately resulted in the origin of earthly matter (Irenaeus, *Refutation* I, 4, 1–2).

At every level the Valentinian system is stamped by a tendency to draw a careful distinction from the basic elements of Christian theology which were already traditional at the time. Here the terms which in the biblical writings and Christian theological reflection denote one and the same authority are divided into several aspects which, as we saw, appear in the framework of a mytho-logical narrative as persons separate in space and time. We can observe this particularly well in the fragmentation of the figure of Jesus Christ. This leads to four separate authorities: first, a 'firstborn' proceeds directly from the Father and the idea that belongs to the Father, who bears the particularly exalted title Christ from the Gospel of John (John 1.14, 18); secondly, after the fall of Sophia the 'fullness' of the 'divine eternities' is completed by a divine eternity named 'Christ', which comes from the 'firstborn'. Thirdly, the creator of the world, the demiurge, comes from the divine eternities Christ and Wisdom – this too is a traditional title of Christ in early Christian theology. And fourthly, a last figure is sent by Christ alone at the level of matter, the 'Paraclete' (in English perhaps 'Comforter') or 'Redeemer', a figure which bears two further titles from the Gospel of John (cf. John 14.26; 4.42). Only for its Christian opponents was this a confusing collection of divine figures and a clear step towards polytheism: of course the Valentinians could explain to their hearers that simply by giving the four authorities titles of Christ they were indicating that these were aspects of one and the same divinity. In the end, all the differentiations merely served to explain how far the one God was connected with the man Jesus of Nazareth and could be designated redeemer of humankind.

The myth also contains an attempt to understand the story of the fall of the first human couple in the Bible (Gen. 3.1–24), which had long been enigmatic, and thus at the same time to give an answer to the question how evil came into God's originally good creation. The fall, which in fact is not really explained by a simple reference to the maliciousness of a serpent and the gullibility of an individual woman, is made comprehensible by its ideal model at the divine level: according to Valentinian teaching, before human beings fall away from God in sin, a part of God, an eternity, falls. This aeon is called 'Wisdom', 'Sophia'. It develops a passion which is really quite appropriate for it: it wants to know God, the unknowable abyss. The problem discussed here was to be debated down the centuries in philosophy as a problem of the knowledge of the self and the perception of the subject, and would be reflected on theoretically at length for the first time in Neoplatonism just a century later: it is already present in the early Christian theology of the second century in the form of a mythological narrative. But since antiquity regarded passion as a bad attitude which hindered knowledge, in the view of the Valentinians the passion for knowledge cut off the divine wisdom from God himself. In this way a model for the fall had been constructed, for the Eve of the biblical story, too, wants only to know and is separated from God by precisely this desire. Just as the figure of Christ appears often in the system, so too the fall is often built into the system: thus the creator of the world, the demiurge, creates the world without a knowledge of the real circumstances and even without knowledge of his own connection with the supreme divine primal father (*Refutation* I, 5, 2).

The 'great system' of the Valentinians also includes an anthropology which, again in the Platonic tradition, understands human beings as divided into three and connects their three elements, 'spirit', 'soul' and 'body', with different divine authorities in creation. Only the spirit, which is implanted in human beings without the knowledge of the creator of the world, who is remote from the 'centre' of God, is saved – through knowledge – whereas the soul, which is made by the creator of the world, and the body, which consists of matter, perishes (*Refutation* I, 5, 6–6, 1). In analogy to these three partial spheres of the human being there are also three groups of people: those who are completely in thrall to the material world and will perish; those who are shaped by the spirit and will one day celebrate the marriage feast with the angels, and finally a middle group whose fate is still open (*Refutation* V, 7, 5). Irenaeus observes that the Valentinians assign ordinary church Christians to the middle group and themselves to the group of those stamped by the spirit. Whether in fact all Valentinians thought that they were saved by nature and could not fall again in life is very questionable.

The Valentinians attempted – to use a graphic metaphor – to make Christianity more competitive in the market of opinions, philosophies and forms of religion by 'expanding' Christian theology, adding a prehistory and a sequel to the Bible. The lack of sources makes it now very difficult to decide whether in so doing they were taking up stimuli from early representatives of 'gnosis' like Saturninus, or whether such a type of doctrine was simply in the air and not the view of a specific group. But it is clear that the great Valentinian system is a classical phase of 'gnosis' in the sense of our typological model: the decisive act of redemption consists in human beings coming to

know that they are ultimately only part of the passions of
the wisdom of God, which is distinct from God, and thus
also perceiving that they are part of God – albeit a remote
part. This system is markedly removed not only from
Valentinus himself but also from classical Platonism by
virtue of its radically pessimistic view of the world and
creation: despite all its recognizable dependence on
Platonic popular philosophy, an educated contemporary
Platonist could only sharply refute it, and in fact we
have such a refutation in writing from the pen of the
Neoplatonic philosopher Plotinus.

Nevertheless, this school of Christian theology evidently
proved very popular: we have a whole series of texts, mythological variants on the system and reports by outsiders from
which the intellectual liveliness of this group is evident.
The last witnesses who can be claimed for the existence of
Valentinians come from the seventh century, but already
after the middle of the fifth century Valentinians no longer
seem to have been a real factor – perhaps because of the
turmoil at the time of the migrations and the consolidation
of the state-church system.

3. The so-called 'Barbelo-gnostics'

Irenaeus also mentions among the representatives of a
developed 'gnosis' a group which today scholars like to call
'Barbelo-gnostics'. Unfortunately the original Greek text of
this section in Irenaeus has not survived. Linguistically, the
beginning in the Latin translation which contains the name
of the group is in some disorder and therefore is difficult to
interpret. But the usual literal rendering of the Latin texts
as 'Barbelo-gnostics' is certainly wrong, since in the later
accounts by early Christian theologians there is never any
mention of 'Barbelo-gnostics' but at most of 'Barbeliotes',
'Barbelo-people' (cf. Epiphanius, *Medicine Chest* II, 26, 3, 7).
The original text of Irenaeus could have stated that from
the group of 'Simonians', whom the author – as I have said
– regards as the first representatives of knowledge falsely

so-called, 'a large number of people sprouted up from the earth like mushrooms who know the "Barbelo"' (*Refutation* I, 29, 1). Of course that was intended as bitter polemic.

According to Irenaeus' report, 'Barbelo' is the name of an eternity of the supreme God who here is also called 'unnameable Father', in order to indicate his sheer inaccessibility (*Refutation* I, 29, 1). In the 'Secret Writing of John' from the Nag Hammadi Library, the authors of which have evidently used the same source that Irenaeus used in the composition of his passage, this unnameable Father is described at some length with negative predicates (*il*limitable, *un*fathomable, *im*measurable, *in*visible, *in*expressible, etc), before the origin of a first divine eternity, the divine idea, is described. This eternity is called 'Barbelo' and the term seems to be an alien body among what are in all nineteen designations of the first divine idea, all of which come from popular philosophy. Irenaeus does not mention the other designations, but begins his report immediately with the enigmatic expression 'Barbelo', in order to cast doubt on the intellectual level of this group from the very beginning. Whatever its original meaning may have been (some suggestions are 'in the four is God' and 'companion of the Lord'), the term belongs in the great mass of Hebrew and Aramaic-sounding secret words with which people in antiquity tried to show the supernatural level of a theological system and the serious nature of magical texts.

The mythological narrative presented in Irenaeus and the 'Secret Writing' differs from the system of the 'Valentinians' first by virtue of its great complexity. But the basic structure corresponds to the Valentinian myth: again eternities arise from the divine mind and the supreme God is supplemented by specific groups of eternities. Again a 'firstborn' comes into being as the conclusion of the self-unfolding of the divine being. At first sight the trinity which arises in this way seems to be a father–mother–son sequence and thus not very Christian. But of course the unknowable Father is no more thought of as 'male' than his thought, the Barbelo, is thought of as 'female'; the 'Secret Writing' also says that quite clearly: 'a male–female eternity' (AJ, BG 28, 2f.). To this degree, while there is indeed an allusion to the metaphor of a one-child family, in the same breath it is energetically dismissed. There is little against understanding this image, which at first sight is so un-Christian, as an attempt to develop intellectually the Christian doctrine of the Trinity of the Father, the Son and the Holy Spirit, then in process of coming into being. Only at a distance of many centuries of theological development does this very archaic attempt seem slightly absurd, and so remote from Christianity that some want to postulate a pre-Christian origin of the triad in Judaism. But we should not deceive ourselves about the intellectual level of such an argument either: similar speculations about the self-unfolding of the divine occur a little later in Plotinus and other Neoplatonists.

However, such a theoretical claim in the system of this 'gnosis' is masked by an immediate delight in the mythological narrative: thus in contrast to the 'Valentinian' model, the process of the self-unfolding of the divine also contains the origin of 'four lights', which are perhaps thought of as the originals of the four well-known archangels Michael, Raphael, Gabriel and Uriel, or represent the four ages of the world. Like the Barbelo, these four lights again bear almost incomprehensible angelic names of Hebrew or Aramaic origin, but for those who know these languages they are distinguished by the syllable '-el' as further immediate partial aspects of God (and are also attested in instructions for magic: Kropp, *Koptische Zaubertexte* I, 22–6): Harmozel, Oroiael, Daveithe and Eleleth. Each of the four lights is further surrounded by three divine eternities – for example, Harmozel by grace, truth and form and Eleleth by perfection, peace and wisdom. Again it is clear even from the names that here, too, as complete an enumeration of divine glory as possible is to be given only in the form of a mythological story, although the supreme God really cannot be described at all. Irenaeus of Lyons and Epiphanius of Salamis time and again pointed out polemically that the many names for the divine authorities in the systems of 'gnosis' are really only 'designations and names for one and the same' (*Refutation* II, 35, 3; cf. *Medicine Chest* II, 26, 10, 11 and 40, 5, 9). They either did not want to understand or in fact did not know that this was to be expressed in the form of mythical discourse as a central concern of almost all systems of 'gnosis'.

The close affinity of the myth of the so-called 'Barbelo-gnostics' to the 'Valentinian' system becomes particularly clear when we investigate how the origin of evil, the creation of the world and the fall of the first man is explained. For again the fall of the divine eternity 'wisdom' and its passionate urge for knowledge is made responsible for all this. And once more an imperfect creator god emerges from this false step who again bears an artificial Semitic name, 'Ialdabaoth', probably to be translated 'begetter of the powers'. We need not pursue the further progress of the myth at this point, because here too it becomes clear that the system is on the one hand constructed, as among the Valentinians, with clear references to popular Platonic maxims and biblical concepts, but on the other integrates terms from magical instructions and peripheral areas of ancient Judaism to a much greater degree than in the case of the systems we have got to know so far.

Sethian gnosis?

As I have already remarked, the expression 'Barbelo-gnostics' is a modern coinage to designate a great system of ancient 'gnosis'. In his report on the myth Irenaeus put the term 'Barbelo' at the centre, but in the 'Secret Writing' it is only one expression in a long chain of designations. Apart from Irenaeus, only Epiphanius mentions a group which are designated 'Barbelites' by the adherents of 'knowledge' (*Medicine Chest* II, 26, 3, 7; cf. also 21, 2, 5). But on the other hand he asserts that a group which derives itself from the Hellenistic Jewish Christian Nicolaus mentioned in the Acts of the Apostles and which he therefore calls the 'Nicolaites'

(Acts 6.5; cf. Rev. 2.2) introduce the 'Barbelo' into their system as the mother of the creator 'Ialdabaoth' (*Medicine Chest* II, 25, 3, 4). Thus hopeless confusion of the ordering and naming of groups brought on to the scene those who were intent on creating order and until modern times has spurred people on to look for the group or school to which the system reported on above is to be attributed.

In the process of the self-unfolding of the deity described in the 'Secret Writing', among the many divine eternities there appear in a very prominent place the 'descendants of Seth', who are also called the 'souls of the holy' (BG 36, 3–5). Modern scholars have connected this report with a group which first Hippolytus and later Epiphanius designate as 'Sethians'. However, what Hippolytus reports as a system of this group (*Refutation* V, 19, 1–21, 12) has little to do with the myth which is developed in extracts in Irenaeus and at length in the 'Secret Writing'. Epiphanius explicitly emphasizes that the 'Sethians' were not very widespread, and cannot even remember in which city of Egypt he encountered them (*Medicine Chest* II, 39, 1, 1). But even the system reported there has only very general similarities to what is unfolded in Irenaeus and the 'Secret Writing'.

Of course it is possible – as Hans-Martin Schenke has proposed – not to start from the early Christian theologians Hippolytus or Epiphanius in defining what present-day scholarly discussion wants to understand by 'Sethian gnosis', but to take together a series of Nag Hammadi writings in which the 'knowers' understand themselves as 'seed of Seth', as descendants of Seth, and at the same time achieve their redemption through knowledge of this descent. In that case the various versions of the 'Secret Writing' and the 'Apocalypse of Adam' (NHC V, 5) or the tractate 'Zostrianos' (NHC VIII, 1) would belong to a modern sub-group of systems of 'gnosis', namely 'Sethian gnosis'. However, in these writings Adam's posthumous son Seth has quite diverse functions: in some writings he functions as a mediator of redemption (e.g. in EvEg, NHC III, 2/IV, 2), in others only as the ancestor of a special spiritual race which is disposed towards knowledge (e.g. in ApcAd, NHC V, 5). Because of these differences, some scholars hesitate to subsume these various systems under the general heading 'Sethian gnosis' and even make this a second main branch of the movement in antiquity alongside 'Valentinian' gnosis (as does B. Layton). They rightly ask whether the identity of any ancient group at all corresponded to the modern construct 'Sethianism'.

But which of the systems presented here is the oldest? So-called 'Valentinian gnosis' or 'Barbelo-gnosis' or 'Sethian gnosis'? The striking common features of course call for an explanation, as do the clear differences. One answer which is still widespread today can be inferred from the work of Irenaeus. He claims that Valentinus was the first to put the outlines 'of the direction of so-called "knowledge"' in the form of a separate school (*Refutation* I, 11, 1). The system of the later so-called 'Barbelo-gnostics' would thus belong, like the systems of Simon, Menander, Saturninus or Basilides, with the presuppositions of the great synthesis of the 'Valentinians', and the clear differences would be explained by a reduction and correction of the wealth of mythology. A critical objection has been made by the French scholar Simone Petrément (*A Separate God*, 1992, 386–429), namely that the sources from which Irenaeus reconstructs the 'Valentinian' system and those 'who know the "Barbelo"' come from about the same time. Mme Petrément has based on these and other observations the opposite thesis, that the 'Valentinian' system is older. For want of clear sources it may be impossible to resolve the question which system is the earlier, and we may have to content ourselves with noting that from the beginning of the second third of the second century very different groups from a whole series of places attempted to express basic features of Jewish-Christian theology against the background of popular Platonic assumptions. These systems differ from one another in characteristic points, but resemble one another in their basic principle: in place of the one God and his Christ, in a mythological narrative virtually any relatively important characteristic of God is stylized as a person, and there is at least one heavenly prehistory or sequel, if not several, to the great theological themes of the fall of man, the origin of evil and the sending of the redeemer Jesus Christ.

Finally, in the third century, we can observe the remarkable phenomenon that clear systems like the Valentinian system 'run wild'. As a result of additions and changes the myth originally told with an eye to popular philosophy, which semi-educated people could read as an answer to fundamental religious and philosophical questions, became incomprehensible: the mythological figures took on a life of their own, and even in such simple processes as the transcription of manuscripts, systems became disordered and went astray. The text 'Pistis Sophia' from the London Codex Askewianus, mentioned above, is a good example of the way in which originally coherent systems 'ran wild'.

V

Manichaeism as the Culmination and Conclusion of 'Gnosis'

Different though the perspectives on the beginnings of the ancient movement which I have tried to reconstruct under the key word 'knowledge' are, there is agreement in the interpretation of the religion which originated from the Persian Mani in the third century and was already designated 'Manichaeism' in the next century. It is not only the conclusion of the development of the great ancient systems of 'gnosis' from a particular interpretation of the Christian tradition to an independent religion, but also an attempt at a deliberate synthesis of previous religion. The significance of the Manichaean mission which reached out as far as China is that through Mani 'the truth of the knowledge that is peculiar to the Father is made visible in the midst of the religions and peoples, to take to himself his own from all' (Cologne Mani Codex, 19, 1–9). Accordingly Manichaeism made use not only of a wealth of languages but also of their religious terminologies to express its concern. From a systematic perspective we see here the great theoretical integrative power in the systems, which finally could break open even the original theoretical framework of reference, namely Christianity. The Manichaeans were adherents of a great and deliberate synthesis of religions which transcended the previous

101

religions, and to this degree also saw themselves as the
better Christians. This is also written in the great doctrinal
work the 'Chapters [*Kephalaia*] of the Teacher' which were
found in 1930 in Medinet Madi (see p. 61). Ten advantages
of the Manichaean religion are stated in Chapter 151 (370,
16, 375, 15 – unfortunately only the text of seven of the
advantages is completely legible); here with words of Mani
the advantages of the Manichaean 'church' – this word
stands for organized religion – over the other 'churches'
are depicted:

- The missionary success of the previous churches was
  limited; the Manichaean mission reaches both the
  East and the West.

- Unlike the holy scriptures of other churches, the
  Manichaeans have not only religious writings but also
  authentic images of wisdom.

- Whereas hitherto the churches only remained for a
  certain time, the Manichaean church will remain to
  the end of the world.

- Just as water flows together with water, so writings,
  wisdom, revelations, parables and psalms of all former
  churches (at another point it becomes clear that here
  the thought is not only of the Judaeo-Christian
  heritage but above all of the religions of Zarathustra
  and Buddha, 7, 31– 8, 7) have 'become a single great
  wisdom' with the writings of Mani and thus surpass
  what has been known hitherto (372, 11–19).

- The persecutions announced by former apostles
  have happened to the Manichaean church and have
  authenticated its preaching. (*The sixth advantage can
  no longer be deciphered.*)

- In the great war which is to come the holy
  Manichaean church will establish itself, whereas
  the others will manifestly perish or have already
  perished. (*The text is damaged.*)

- The other 'former churches' will not withstand the
  coming persecutions of the false Christ, whereas

the Manichaean church will become established. (*The texts of the ninth and tenth advantages are also so damaged that a reliable reconstruction cannot be made of them.*)

Unlike teachers of the second century like Saturninus, Basilides or Valentinus, about whose biography we can say virtually nothing, and in clear contrast to the usually anonymous authors of the Nag Hammadi writings, a whole romance can be told about the life of the founder of this religious synthesis.

1. The life of Mani

In all probability Mani was born on 14 April 216 in Seleucia-Ctesiphon on the Tigris in present-day Iraq, and spoke Aramaic as well as Persian. His father was a member of a Jewish-Christian baptist sect in southern Mesopotamia, as we can now discover from the Cologne Mani Codex. There we can also read how already in his youth the future founder of a religion became aware of the suffering of vegetables, which cried out and bled when a baptist cut them in the garden for a meal (10, 1–11). While Mani still belonged to this community, according to this source his heavenly twin or companion (Greek *syzygos*) appeared to him to prepare him by visions for his role as revealer. After another vision, at the age of 24 Mani left the baptist community, which in the Cologne Mani Codex is called the 'error of the sectarians' (19, 12f.). After a short phase of discouragement he accepted the call as 'apostle of light', 'come from the land of Babel, so that I should issue a call in the world' (Turfan text M4), to carry on a mission in Mesopotamia, Persia, Media and Azerbaijan as far as India. On this mission Mani was always accompanied by his heavenly companion and two further members of the baptist community. First of all he evidently carried on the mission in his own family, with success: 'When they had heard it, they were converted' (M49 II). The Cologne biography gives a colourful account of Mani's missionary journeys, healing miracles, a journey through the air and the conversion of a king – perhaps the Turan-shah of Turan in present-day Belukhistan north of the mouth of the Indus, who in a vision is taken on a kind of heavenly journey (Berlin Turfan Texts XI, text 2, 2); the successes of the mission are documented in the tradition of Manichaean literature, which is rich. However, the biography also reports difficult conflicts, for example with the Jews of Mesopotamia, who were very interested in magic (137–9). Mani is said to have been called back from India by the Persian great king Shapuhr I (*Kephalaia* 1, 15, 27–16, 2), presumably in AD 242. Initially the religion enjoyed great freedom in the Sassanid kingdom, until the influential priests of the Zoroastrian religion began to fear the competition from it. Mani was arrested under a new great king, Vahram I, and executed on 26 February 277 after a long imprisonment. Since according to the practice of the time his body was mutilated and put on show, his followers saw this as a passion and crucifixion comparable to the end of the life of Jesus Christ.

Mani composed seven works (there is also a list in *Kephalaia* 148, 355, 8–17): the 'Book of Shapuhr' (Shapuhragan), the 'Living Gospel', a 'picture book' which went with it containing large-format illustrations of the Manichaean myth, the 'Treasure of Life', the 'Book of Mysteries', 'Legends', and finally the 'Book of Giants'. He also wrote letters, songs and prayers, all in Aramaic. Only the Shapuhragan was composed in Middle Persian, in homage to the Persian great king Shapuhr, since this was his mother tongue. Mani's disciples produced above all hymns and 'teaching chapters', the so-called *Kephalaia*.

2. The teachings of Mani

The person of Mani and the authority of his revelation is part of the teaching. Mani insisted that like Paul he received his religion – which he called 'hope' (cf. Eph. 1.18) – 'not from human beings or fleshly creatures nor through dealings with scriptures' (Cologne Mani Codex 64,

8–15; cf. Gal. 1.1). So his 'Gospel', too, begins very much like a letter of the apostle Paul:

> I, Mani, an apostle of Jesus Christ by the will of God, the Father of truth, from whom I am, who lives and abides in all eternity, who was before all and will be after all (Version of the Mani Codex, 66, 4–12; Middle Persian in M17).

In Mani, the claim to be conveying a direct revelation of God does not seem to have been imposed on a mythological narrative at a later stage – an impression which we often get in the Nag Hammadi find – but in the Cologne biography is supported by reports of visions. However, Mani was not just a prophet but also a theologian, who tried to offer a rational account of his teachings. That already becomes clear from probably the most prominent Manichaean in the western half of the Roman empire: at an earlier stage of his life, as a teacher of rhetoric in Carthage between 373 and 382, the North African theologian and later bishop Augustine (AD 354–430) belonged to the Manichaeans, on the lower level of a 'hearer'. If we may trust his later statements, he chose this religion especially because of its rationality, and evidently commended it as a higher form of Christianity. Only later did he feel deceived in these expectations (*Confessions* V, 6, 10–7, 13).

The Manichaean myth with its many emanations of God and anti-God was and is difficult to commit to memory, so it was summed up in groups of images and assimilated to the individual world of religious ideas of the religions in the area in which the mission was being carried on. However, Mani's teachings corresponded fully to the typological model which I have used as a basis so far; therefore at this point a quite general survey is sufficient. Mani radicalized into a fundamental dualism the dualism between a good principle and an evil principle which was already suggested in the preceding systems of the second and third centuries. The redeemed knower knows that these two 'did not come forth from one another or ... from One' (*Kephalaia* 3, 23, 2f.) and therefore cannot be derived from an ultimate unity. The 'Letter on Foundations' of the North African

Manichaeans, which is perhaps identical with a letter or discourse by Mani (Fragment 5a, Feldmann), says that 'God the Father rules over the light, eternal in his holy origin'. The Father is surrounded by an incalculable number of eternities, aeons (ibid.), but in contrast to the system of the 'Valentinians' these are not thought of as partial aspects of the one God but as further gods. Whether or not the realm of darkness is ruled by a 'monstrous ruler' (ibid., Fragment 6, Feldmann) or is represented rather by impersonal matter (Greek *hyle*) is one of the fascinating questions in the interpretation of this system.

Central to the progress of the myth is the battle between the two elements which is started by the darkness. Since in this battle the light first of all succumbs for tactical reasons and is imprisoned in evil matter, a mixture of good and evil comes about. The 'Father of light' has the world created from the bodies of the evil demons – inhabitants of the realm of darkness – now mixed with good parts; the world thus represents a mixture of light and darkness. It is not radically evil, but more a place of purification. The task now is to restore the initial state in which good and evil, light and darkness, stood over against each other separately and unmixed, by reversing the process of mixing. To this end light apostles appear, and Mani is merely the last of this chain of apostles, which begins with Adam and extends through the Old Testament patriarchs, Zoroaster, Buddha, Jesus Christ and Paul to the present. Just as the primordial man is redeemed from matter, so too the rest of the particles of light must take their course from the earth through the Milky Way to the moon, and from there to the sun (an originally Stoic idea).

Therefore Manichaeism is characterized by an abrupt repudiation of those elements of this world which represent the darkness and a careful attention to the particles of light in the world. For example, the Cologne Mani Codex says of the 'disgusting flesh and its drunkenness' (22, 12–13) that despite all efforts at religious purity 'blood, gall, wind, shameful excrement and impurity of the body' proceed from food (81, 10–13). True purity is possible only through knowledge, which consists in the separation of the light from the darkness and death from life (84, 9–14). Accordingly Mani's doctrine is characterized by a particularly strict ethic. Fasting, praying and almsgiving – a triad familiar from the Jewish-Christian tradition (cf. Tobit 12.8; Matt. 6.2–18) – are only the first work that the person instructed in Manichaeism has to do (*Kephalaia* 80, 129, 29f.). The 'elect' (*electi*) had to abstain from sexual intercourse, marriage, eating meat and drinking wine, from maltreating plants and polluting water, so as not to damage the particles of life in them; their life was governed by an abundance of prescriptions and rules. Thus the 'elect' is, for example, also to learn to hold his hands in reverent calm (ibid., 129, 9f.). To enable this group to survive – in the end they were not allowed even to cut the leaf of a vegetable – they had to be looked after, as in a hive of bees, by a kind of drone, the 'hearers' (*auditores*). Their gifts were called 'alms' (thus usually according to the Coptic word; the Greek means 'given out of compassion'). So the 'elect' could accept the gifts because they themselves did not have to destroy the living souls in them. The 'hearers' were comforted by being told that they had done this for a holy purpose (*Kephalaia* 93, 236, 24–7). The strict regulations were supplemented by a strict discipline of confession and penance, because sin was regarded as the real manifestation of the kingdom of darkness. Fragments both of a penitential book for the 'elect' in Soghdic (M801, 619–701 and 749–67) and a rule for confession for the 'hearers' in Ugrian, the X^{u}āstvānīft, have been preserved. In this work, for example unwitting sins against human beings, animals, birds, fish and reptiles are addressed:

> If we ever, my God, in any way caused fear or terror to these five kinds of living beings, from the greatest to the smallest; if we ever inflicted on them in any way a blow or cut, or killed them in any way, then we are to the same degree guilty of taking the life of living beings. Therefore we now pray you, my God, to be free from sin. Remit my sin! (V C, based on the translation by J. P. Asmussen).

By contrast, as a third-century letter from Egypt shows, normal church Christians regarded such a defence against the charge of having damaged creation 'as the work of a person who is utterly deluded' (Rylands Papyrus 469).

There was a strict hierarchy in the Manichaean church. After the head of the church, i.e. Mani, and his followers, the church, dispersed over many countries, was ruled by 12 teachers, 72 bishops and 360 presbyters. As far as we can reconstruct it, in the initial stage above all rich merchants and similar professional groups belonged to the new religion – in the end the 'elect' were forbidden to have any fixed abode and had to go through the world preaching. That explains the statement that the 'elect' in the church are like a dough, like 'gods' (*Kephalaia* 149, 357,10–12). But at the same time it is impossible for anyone who has been baptized with water among the Christians to attain the 'kingdom of heaven' without being converted to Manichaeism (ibid., 130, 308, 11–16). Since from AD 302 onwards the Manichaeans were already a secret society because of imperial persecution in the Roman empire, the threshold of entry was raised through the obligation to convert.

The Manichaean religion fell victim to the Mongol attack in the fifteenth century, having still been a powerful influence in the early Middle Ages, above all in the East. Yet in a way it has remained alive to the present day: time and again members of different movements have been accused of being Manichaeans – for example on the basis of a dualistic option – although no historical connections can be made, above all between the mediaeval Cathars active in southern France and the Manichaeans, except for the fact that Christian theologians regarded them from the perspective of Augustine's polemic against the Manichaeans. Presumably Manichaeism has remained fascinating even down to the present day not least because it replaces the known religions of antiquity with a kind of universal religion which at the same time integrated and transcended both Buddhism and Zoroastrianism, and Judaism and Christianity. Thus in a sense it formed a way which was then taken by modern thinkers to rescue religion generally in the face of the Enlightenment critique of the historical religions.

VI

Ancient Communities of 'Gnostics'?

Because the sources are very difficult to use, it is hardly possible really to add any depth to the picture of the ancient systems of 'gnosis', which is primarily presented in terms of the history of ideas. We cannot depict its social history and the history of its various mentalities. The pictures of 'gnosis' which have come down to us from antiquity are too like snapshots overpainted with polemic for us to be able to fit them together into an overall view or even to incorporate them into a history of its development. Moreover we must not overestimate the size and the influence of the movement: for example, Epiphanius refers in great detail in his *Medicine Chest* to the sect of the 'Archontics'; he gives the titles of sacred books which they use and describes their system (II, 40, 1, 1–7, 6). But he can name only a single representative of this group, a hermit, who lived in the neighbourhood of his monastery in Palestine, along with another disciple elsewhere who had perhaps already died. Thus here a veritable group of 'gnosis' proves to be the one-man business of an obscure fourth-century hermit.

However, despite such problems with the reports that have survived, it is possible to make a few basic observations on our theme.

'Knowledge', as I understand it here, developed in precisely the opposite direction from Christianity generally:

whereas Christianity came into being in the first third of
the first century as a rural movement within Judaism, in
little villages in northern Galilee, and only in the course
of the second century established itself in the great cities of
antiquity like Rome, Alexandria or Antioch, early 'gnosis'
was more of an urban phenomenon. We heard of thinkers
in the three great metropolises of antiquity – Rome,
Alexandria and Antioch – and Irenaeus reported gnostic
groups in the trading city of Lyons in Gaul. Biblical
traditions which are difficult to understand in an urban
setting were either explained and translated, like the
expression 'Messiah' in the Gospel of Philip (Saying 19:
NHC II, 3, 104, 3–13; cf. also 53, 111, 21–4), or like the
almost incomprehensible 'magical words' were integrated
without being translated, precisely because of their alien
nature. Later, as 'knowledge' increasingly distanced itself
from Christianity, it turned more into a rural movement,
because its representatives retreated from the cities into the
less conspicuous rural districts. Thus at the end of late
antiquity 'knowledge' embarked on a general retreat and
was able to survive the death or the transformation of the
great cities.

If we are to understand the sociological profile of this
movement, we must initially keep to the figures about
which we still know most, namely the teachers and
theologians. According to all that we know, they correspond to the image that we also get of other Christian
teachers of this time. In both manner and clothing they
imitated above all the itinerant popular philosophers who
gave lectures for money. That has already been conjectured
of the opponents contested by the First Letter to Timothy
whose 'knowledge' is denied them (cf. 1 Tim. 6.5). We
know that Justin or Tertullian wore the traditional clothing
of philosophers (cf. Justin, *Dialogue with Trypho* 1, 2 and 9,
2): cloak, light sandals, stick and goatee beard. For a small
sum of money one could hear lectures from such itinerant
philosophers on central questions of religious and moral
lifestyle: these lectures were given either in public places
like baths, or in private rooms. The level of such lectures is

best described with the term 'popular philosophy', which
has already become familiar to us. There is nothing to
prevent us imagining the early representatives of 'gnosis' as
teaching above all in this way. In the course of the late
second and early third centuries Christianity profession-
alized its teaching and made efforts to form permanent
schools with a regular teaching programme and a way of
life shared by students and teachers – as was customary in
the sphere of professional philosophical teaching above
the level of popular philosophy. Such institutions were
usually financed by money from pupils or by donations. We
do not know whether the systems of 'gnosis' formed in the
early third century were also connected with such profes-
sionalizations of teaching; however, that is improbable,
because the formation of doctrinal systems never reached
the professional level of specialist philosophical or scientific knowledge which slowly but surely begins to become
customary in other forms of Christian theology. Evidently
the adherents of the systems of 'gnosis' gathered as a small
circle of 'knowers' around the charismatic free teachers, as
a small but active conventicle led by intellectuals. Thus in
terms of organizational sociology they remained at the level
of second-century Christian theology generally and did not
make a major move towards professionalization in the third
century, presumably because at this point they had
already been repudiated by most Christian communities
as 'heretics'.

But what did the everyday life of such groups in
which the 'knowers' inside and outside the Christian
communities gathered look like? First of all its central
feature will have been meetings and contact with a charismatic teacher. Presumably the teacher explained the
particularly sacred religious myth in which this system had
been briefly enciphered in accordance with the relevant
laws of construction, commented on the myth in lectures,
but also put questions to the audience; there would have
been disputations over the correct answer. The author of
the First Letter to Timothy already caricatures this style of
meeting in an unfriendly way as 'a morbid craving for

controversy and for disputes about words' (1 Tim. 6.4). In most of the other reports that we possess, whole strata of polemic obscure the little historical information. This applies particularly to the elements of group life which were not connected with lectures and discussions and above all to communal life, meals and liturgical celebrations. In antiquity such a communal life was one of the presuppositions of communal philosophical reflection which was taken for granted.

A little information has survived, but it can hardly be used for historical reconstruction. Thus in his *Medicine Chest* Epiphanius reports on a meal of a group which he designates as 'knowing', in which he possibly took part personally: first of all the men tickled the women and the women the men by rubbing the index finger on the inside of the hand on meeting. This scene has such clearly erotic undertones that at this point we already have to doubt the credibility of the whole report (*Medicine Chest* II, 26, 4, 2). Even in antiquity people greeted one another either with a firm handshake or by embracing and kissing. In like manner the report continues to collect clearly ambiguous information about the meal of the 'knowers'. Epiphanius depicts an orgiastic meal, the details of which present such a sharp contrast with the ideals of the life of a monk of late antiquity that on reading it, even as a lay psychologist, one asks whether here we do not have some of the author's suppressed fantasies.

Although the group is poor, it puts a wealth of food and drink on the table. After feeding abundantly from this table the men say to their wives, 'Arise and make love with your brother' (26, 4, 4). The particular point of this vocabulary only becomes evident in the Greek: the word does not really denote a passionate, sexual love but a sober love in the sense of appreciation or friendly welcome, and among Christians became a technical term for the so called 'love feast' between brothers and sisters, the special form of communal meal among the early Christians. But a writing in the New Testament already engages in polemic against people who are 'blemishes on your love feasts' because they 'boldly carouse together', and concludes: 'for them the nether gloom of darkness has been reserved for ever' (Jude 12f.). Another alleged practice of these 'knowers' reported by Epiphanius seems like a parody of what was customary in the Christian church: after sexual intercourse meant only to provide sheer pleasure and not lead to the procreation of children, men and women offered the male semen like the eucharistic gifts, with hands raised to heaven and even used the relevant liturgical words, 'We offer to you this gift, the body of Christ.' Thereupon they ate what was thus offered, saying: 'That is the body of Christ and that is the paschal lamb through which our bodies suffer and are compelled to confess the suffering of Christ' (26, 4, 5f.). They spoke over menstrual blood the saying over the blood of Christ which belongs in the church's eucharist (26, 4, 8). At another point Epiphanius says that this prayer was offered naked, as a way of finding 'openness to God'. From the perspective of a monk who devotes himself day and night to asceticism and thus to fasting and sexual continence, the description of these obscene practices culminates with the charge that here 'day and night the body is tended' with ointments and baths, with food and drink (26, 5, 8). Epiphanius' assertion that the 'knowers' chopped stillborn babies in pieces, crushed them in a mortar and made them edible with honey, pepper, perfumes and herbs, so that everyone from the circle could eat the crushed embryo with their fingers (26, 5, 4), fits perfectly into the realm of ancient horror stories about various groups which people were fond of telling. We can derive virtually nothing from such horror stories for reconstructing the everyday life of 'knowers'; on the contrary, 'gnostic' texts like the 'Pistis Sophia' protest against people 'who take male seed and female menstrual blood and put it in a lentil dish and eat it'. The 'Pistis Sophia' makes Jesus say that such people 'will be consumed and destroyed in the outermost darkness' (251, 14–17, 23–5). There is also polemic in the 'Books of Jeû' against such people, who are supposed to have said at their obscene meal: 'We have attained the true knowledge and pray to the true God' (304, 19f.).

What the North African theologian Tertullian writes about the everyday life of 'knowers' has equally marked polemical colouring. He mentions an assembly:

> They meet together, listen to one another, pray with one another. Even if non-Christians attend, they cast the holy to the dogs and pearls, though false ones, to the swine ... They are all conceited, they all promise 'knowledge'. The catechumens are 'perfect' even before they have been taught. Even the heretical women – how brazen they are! – are bold enough to teach and to discuss, to perform exorcisms, to promise healings, perhaps even to baptize (Tertullian, *The Indictment against the Heretics* 41).

However, there are not many references to 'equal rights' for women in the movement, and we also find all kinds of evidence of a disparagement of women, like the notorious Saying 114 of the Gospel of Thomas from Nag Hammadi (NHC II, 2, 51, 24–5): 'Every woman who will make herself male will enter the kingdom of heaven.'

It is particularly difficult to discover the liturgical life of the groups whose history and systems I have described. Since in the second and third centuries Christian worship took place in houses which prominent members of the community made available for this purpose, and not in special rooms for worship, many members of the groups will simply have taken part in the normal worship of the house churches to which they belonged anyway. But probably individual groups also formed such house churches (cf. Irenaeus, *Refutation* I, 13, 3). Only at the point when the movement increasingly markedly parted company with Christianity, or Christianity separated itself from the groups as part of the process of its consolidation, was there a need to offer separate worship. Unfortunately we know virtually nothing about the form of such worship, and the little that we do know hardly takes us any further. The Gospel of Philip mentions in Saying 68 the sacraments of 'baptism, chrism, eucharist, redemption and bridal chamber' (67, 28–30). The context makes it quite clear that all five sacraments had the same theological status. Thus alongside baptism, accompanied by anointing with oil (cf. 74, 12–15), and the Lord's Supper, which according to ancient custom was called 'thanksgiving' (*eucharistia*) after a partial aspect of the celebration of the meal, there were also the sacraments of 'redemption' and 'the bridal chamber'. This last term alludes to a detail of the primal heavenly redemption in the 'Valentinian' system, namely the final return of the fallen divine eternity 'Wisdom' into the divine fullness, which is described as a wedding. Was this primal image imitated? How was the wedding performed? What effects were promised from it? Or did the normal incorporation into the community take place on Easter Day, when baptism, anointing and the first eucharist took place, interpreted along with the rest of Christianity as the beginning of redemption and the symbolic anticipation of the bridal chamber? In that case the series of sacraments mentioned would merely provide a higher interpretation for the 'normal' ceremonial baptism of any Christian. However, unfortunately we do not know anything about the form of these sacraments, not even whether they were elements of a rite of initiation into the group (thus Irenaeus, *Refutation* I, 21, 3). But the small number of accounts at least justifies us in conjecturing that the worship of groups of 'knowers' would hardly have differed from that of other Christians – otherwise such accounts of obscene celebrations of the eucharist among the 'gnostics' of the kind that we find in Epiphanius would not have had to have been invented. However, we can assume that some texts from the Nag Hammadi Library and the Coptic texts previously known were used in liturgical contexts.

Now time and again attempts have been made to connect the origin of the movement with particular political and social factors. Here reference has been made to Max Weber, who produced the formula: 'Any need for redemption is the expression of a "need", and social or economic oppression is by no means the exclusive source of its origin, though of course it is a very important one' (*Wirtschaft und Gesellschaft 2: Religiöse Gemeinschaften* [MWG I/22-2], 2001, 253). However, the origin of systems of 'knowledge' and especially the rise of the feeling of alienation and pessimism about the world with which these systems are stamped cannot be related specifically to an economic or political depression. On the contrary, the second century must be seen as having been a particularly prosperous period of ancient history. At all events, as we saw, the situation in individual parts of the empire which was oppressive for Christians, and which only to a very limited degree corresponded to the forecasts for the future in the New Testament writings, may be considered as a possible cause of such 'darkening'. For want of sources, how far that radically pessimistic view of the world and the creation of the world held by many systems helped people to overcome uncertainties in their own existence – whether individual or collective – must remain open: but quite certainly the early period of the empire was not an 'age of anxiety' (contra Eric Robertson Dodds, 1965).

Weber and others after him also put forward the view that the old middle class of the Eastern provinces of the empire had been stripped of power by the Roman occupation of further parts of the ancient world and thus depoliticized (*Wirtschaft und Gesellschaft*, 270). They developed into a radically apolitical intellectual stratum which with the new conditions also rejected the world as a whole. But on closer analysis this sociological explanation of the origin of the great systems, too, does not really stand up: in the provinces the traditional structures and élites were largely left to function and perform the tasks they had performed previously. In the time of the empire these political units were governed with a minimal administrative and military apparatus of imperial officials and thus largely in co-operation with indigenous officials. The common notion that Christians in particular would have been excluded from political and military offices because of their confession is, though, inaccurate: that may have been the case in some parts of the empire, but in others we have very early evidence of Christians in a variety of political and military positions. The correct element in Weber's observations remains that the systems formed in the second and third centuries were constructed by intellectuals for intellectuals (if we are willing to transfer to antiquity in an anachronistic way a term which bears the stamp of clearly later times). In so doing, on the one hand they helped Christianity to have an influence on the educated society of the time and on the other aided a 'privatization' of the new religion: it is in the nature of an 'intellectual' also to have an interest in avoiding conflicts. So those who regarded themselves as 'knowers' attempted to avoid conflicts within the Christian community by presenting their own theory as a higher form of the Christianity of the community. Conflicts with the non-Christian environment would in any case have been avoided by the deliberate orientation on current standards in religion and popular philosophy. However, we have seen in the case of Platonism that this hope of avoiding conflict presumably proved disappointing: the Platonists did not accept the Platonizing of Christianity undertaken here. This fact must explain why the adherents of the systems of 'knowledge' soon no longer consisted of highly-educated intellectuals, but were made up of more ordinary people. The way in which the systems 'ran wild' in the third century, which I have described (pp. 99f.), is a literary reflection of this process. This picture finds confirmation in Augustine's reports on the intellectual level of the Manichaean bishops in the fourth century, which cannot simply be dismissed as polemic.

VII

'Gnosis' in Antiquity and the Present

Time and again I have interpreted the doctrines and systems that on the basis of my typological model I assigned to ancient 'gnosis' as an attempt to make Christianity and its specific world-view understandable to semi-educated contemporaries and thus competitive in a religious market of possibilities. An effort was made with contemporary scholarly methods, for example biblical philology or philosophical argument, as far as people were capable of this, to formulate Christian answers to the great religious questions of the time. In particular, an attempt was made to tell a myth based on a Platonic model which supplemented the biblical stories with those parts which in the opinion of many educated people were lacking.

Of course we can ask whether, in this attempt to supplement the biblical tradition, so many elements from popular Platonism and traditional material from the magical texts and particular special forms of Judaism were introduced that the genuine biblical elements were gradually suppressed. What remains of the person of the man Jesus of Nazareth if at the same time he appears on four levels of the divine process as a figure? Accordingly, after the expulsion of Marcion from the community in the city of Rome, Christian theologians, too, formulated increasingly precise standards for correct Christian theology and thus excluded the systems of 'gnosis' from

Christian theology. As a result the systems increasingly also adopted anti-Christian polemic and 'gnosis' began to constitute itself a separate religion. This development came to a conclusion in Manichaeism.

However, we can understand this process correctly only if we become clear that the rise of the early schemes of 'gnosis' and the origin of its great 'systems' falls in a great revolutionary period in the history of Christianity. Within a few decades a movement which had originally come into being in very small villages on the north shore of a lake in the north of a remote province of the Roman empire, and which moreover was utterly focused on its Jewish context, spread through the great cities and cultural metropolises all over the empire with explosive force. Initially it was barely equipped for this process of transformation: its adherents were fishermen, toll collectors or experts in the exegesis of the Jewish law, not scholars or philosophers who could have explained the advantages of the new religion to educated non-Jews. So we must understand the second century as a kind of laboratory in which, in very different corners of the empire, as it were experiments were being made by very different individuals with very different gifts in an attempt to arrive at a Christian theology which was competitive on the market of ancient world-views. Many theologians, and by no means only those whom I have assigned to 'gnosis', experimented with notions from popular Platonism; but most professional Platonic philosophers were quite disturbed by the results. Some theologians evidently explored the world of the names used in magical incantation and wanted to integrate them into their system in order to win people over; presumably professional magicians simply laughed at that. The attempt by Christian theologians to explain Christianity to their contemporaries by systems of 'gnosis' led away from Christianity. We might almost say that the professional risk in a laboratory is that occasionally the equipment may fly around one's ears.

But this is the view of a Christian theologian. Anyone who follows the course of systems of 'gnosis' beyond antiquity will by no means want to speak simply of the failure of this scheme of a very special philosophy of religion, but on the contrary must note time and again the attractiveness of the ideas brought together in our typological model. Carl Gustav Jung (1875–1961) is a particularly prominent twentieth-century example of this. Jung, who was fond of being photographed with an ancient 'gnostic ring', an amulet with the depiction of a magical being on it, not only wrote about gnosis but even produced a gnostic myth himself. In 1916, at the age of 41, he wrote a visionary tractate under the title *Septem Sermones ad mortuos* ('Seven sermons on the dead'), which he later disowned as a 'sin of his youth'. He did not write this text under his own name but used the pseudonym of the early 'gnostic' Basilides, and like the so-called 'Barbelo-gnostics' combined in his text elements from the ancient systems of 'gnosis' and magical instructions. Similarly, at present very different groups are fascinated by the ancient myths: thus the wealth of images which are used to describe the divine being attract people who for many reasons are critical of the traditional Christian discourse about God – for example, because here more feminine images are used than in the sober language of the ancient philosophies of antiquity which Christian theology took over. The concept of describing redemption as self-knowledge also contin-ually proves attractive. Every shelf of esoteric literature at the present day contains better and worse examples of the topicality of a phenomenon the early history of which I have described.

Nevertheless the present effect of 'gnosis' is not limited to the 'Body, Mind and Spirit' shelves of bookshops. Nor is it exhausted in the rediscovery of particular texts of this movement in individual trends of Christian piety, above all in the United States. The new interest in 'gnosis' extends as far as the philosophical faculties of German universities. Hans Blumenberg had already made ancient 'gnosis' and its repudiation of the world a key in his own great interpret-ation of modernity and claimed that 'Modernity is the overcoming of gnosis' (*The Legitimacy of the Modern Age,*

1983). Whereas the 'repudiation of gnosis' does not take place in the theological system of Augustine and in mediaeval scholasticism or, if it does, demands a high price, in modernity affirmation of the world and coping with the world replaces the gnostic repudiation of the world. This view is in turn contradicted by other philosophers: for Peter Koslowski, by contrast, modernity is an era of secularized 'gnosis' (he speaks of 'gnosticism': *Gnosis und Mystik in der Geschichte der Philosophie*, 1988, 391): current crises of the technological age are compared, for example, with the provocation of the gnostic demiurge.

In this short book, only a relatively brief attempt has been made to understand a difficult phenomenon of ancient intellectual history with the aid of a typological model. Of course such matter-of-fact analyses only make a beginning of explaining why the ancient systems of 'gnosis' still fascinate people so much. Perhaps the uninterrupted fascination owes itself not least to the fact that the great questions to which these systems attempt to give an answer in a very specific way still oppress people as much as they did many centuries ago, despite all assertions to the contrary. If that were the case, the thesis of an increasing secularization of society in modernity would once again have to be examined very thoroughly.

The Nag Hammadi Codices

NHC	Column/line	Abbreviation	Title
I, 1	A, 1–B, 10	PrecPl	The Prayer of the Apostle Paul
I, 2	1, 1–16, 30	EpJac	The Letter of James
I, 3	16, 31–43, 24	EV	The Gospel of Truth
I, 4	43, 25–50, 18	Rheg	The Letter to Rheginus on the Resurrection
I, 5	51, 1–138, 27	TracTrip	The Tripartite Tractate
II, 1	1, 1–32, 9	AJ	The Apocryphon of John
II, 2	32, 10–51, 28	EvThom	The Gospel of Thomas
II, 3	51, 29–86, 19	EvPhil	The Gospel of Philip
II, 4	86, 20–97, 23	HA	The Hypostasis of the Archons
II, 5	97, 24–127, 17	OW	The Origin of the World

NHC	Column/line	Abbreviation	Title
II, 6	127,18–137, 27	ExAn	The Exegesis on the Soul
II, 7	138, 1–145, 19	LibThom	The Book of Thomas
III, 1	1, 1–40, 11	AJ	The Apocryphon of John
III, 2	40, 12–69, 20	EvEg	The Gospel of the Egyptians
III, 3	70, 1–90, 13	Eug	The Letter of Eugnostos
III, 4	90, 14–119, 18	SJC	The Sophia of Jesus Christ
III, 5	120, 1–147, 23	Dial	The Dialogue of the Saviour
IV, 1	1, 1–49, 28	AJ	The Apocryphon of John
IV, 2	50, 1–81, 2	EvEg	The Gospel of the Egyptians
V, 1	1, 1–17, 18	Eug	The Letter of Eugnostos
V, 2	17, 19–24, 9	ApcPl	The Apocalypse of Paul
V, 3	24, 10–44, 10	1ApcJac	The First Apocalypse of James
V, 4	44, 11–63, 32	2ApcJac	The Second Apocalypse of James
V, 5	64, 1–85, 32	ApcAd	The Apocalypse of Adam
VI, 1	1, 1–12, 22	ActPet	The Acts of Peter and the Twelve Apostles
VI, 2	13, 1–21, 32	Bronte	Thunder: Perfect Mind

NHC	Column/line	Abbreviation	Title
VI, 3	22, 1–35, 24	AuthLog	The Original Teaching
VI, 4	36, 1–48, 15	Noema	The Concept of our Great Power
VI, 5	48, 16–51, 23		Plato, *Republic* 588b–589B
VI, 6	52, 1–63, 32	OgdEnn	On the Eighth and the Ninth
VI, 7	63, 33–65, 7	PrecHerm	Hermetic Prayer
VI, 8	65, 15–78, 43	Ascl	Asclepius
VII, 1	1, 1–49, 9	ParShem	The Paraphrase of Shem
VII, 2	49, 10–70, 12	2LogSeth	The Second Logos of the Great Seth
VII, 3	70, 13–84, 14	ApcPet	The Apocalypse of Peter
VII, 4	84, 15–118, 7	Silv	The Teachings of Silvanus
VII, 5	118, 10–127, 2	StelSeth	The Three Steles of Seth
VIII, 1	1, 1–132, 6	Zostr	Zostrianos
VIII, 2	132, 10–140, 27	EpPet	The Letter of Peter to Philip
IX, 1	1, 1–27, 10	Melch	Melchizedek
IX, 2	27, 11–29, 5	OdNor	The Ode on Norea
IX, 3	29, 6–74, 30	TestVer	The Testimony of Truth
X, 1	1, 1–68, 18	Mars	Marsanes
XI, 1	1, 1–21, 35	Inter	The Interpretation of Knowledge
XI, 2	22, 1–39, 39	ExpVal	A Valentinian Exposition

NHC	Column/line	Abbreviation	Title
XI, 2A	40, 1–44, 37	PrecVal	Five Valentinian Prayers
XI, 3	45, 1–69, 20	Allog	Allogenes
XI, 4	69, 21–72, 33	Hyps	Hypsiphrone
XII, 1	15, 1–34, 28	Sextus	The Sentences of Sextus
XII, 2	53, 19–60, 30	EV	The Gospel of Truth
XII, 3			Fragments
XIII, 1	35, 1–50, 24	Protennoia	The Trimorphic Protennoia
XIII, 2	50, 25ff.	OW	The Origin of the World (fragment)

The Berlin Coptic Papyrus

NHC	Column/line	Abbreviation	Title
8502, 1	7, 1–19, 5	EvMar	The Gospel of Mary
8502, 2	19, 6–77, 7	AJ	The Apocryphon of John
8502, 3	77, 8–127, 12	SJC	The Sophia of Jesus Christ
8502, 4	128, 1–141, 7	ActumPet	The Act of Peter

Abbreviations

General abbreviations

BG	Berlin Coptic Papyrus
CH	Corpus Hermeticum
CIL	Corpus Inscriptionum Latinarum
Cramer	Catenae Graecorum Patrum in Novum Testamentum (Oxford 1943 = Hilversum 1967; a collection of fragments of ancient Christian commentaries on the Bible)
NHC	Nag Hammadi Codices (= writings from the Nag Hammadi Library)
NHS	Nag Hammadi Studies
NHMS	Nag Hammadi and Manichaean Studies

Abbreviations of biblical books

Gen.	Genesis
Ex.	Exodus
Ps.	Psalms
Prov.	Proverbs
Isa.	Isaiah
Ezek.	Ezekiel
Hos.	Hosea
Sir.	Jesus Sirach

Wisd.	Wisdom of Solomon
Matt.	Gospel of Matthew
Mark	Gospel of Mark
Luke	Gospel of Luke
John	Gospel of John
Acts	Acts of the Apostles
Rom.	Letter to the Romans
1 Cor.	First Letter to the Corinthians
2 Cor.	Second Letter to the Corinthians
Gal.	Letter to the Galatians
Eph.	Letter to the Ephesians
Col.	Letter to the Colossians
1 Tim.	First Letter to Timothy
Rev.	Revelation of John

Abbreviations of the gnostic writings of the Nag Hammadi Library

ActPet	The Acts of Peter and the Twelve Apostles (NHC VI, 1)
AJ	The Apocryphon of John (NHC II, 1)
Allog	Allogenes (NHC XI, 3)
ApcAd	The Apocalypse of Adam (NHC V, 5)
1 ApcJac	The First Apocalypse of James (NHC V, 3)
2 ApcJac	The Second Apocalypse of James (NHC V, 4)
ApcPl	The Apocalypse of Paul (NHC V, 2)
ApcPet	The Apocalypse of Peter (NHC VII, 3)
Ascl	Asclepius (NHC VI, 8)
AuthLog	(*Authentikos Logos*) The Original Teaching (NHC VI, 3)
Bronte	(*Bronte*) Thunder: Perfect Mind (NHC VI, 2)
Dial	The Dialogue of the Saviour (NHC III, 5)
EpJac	The Letter of James (NHC I, 2)
EpPet	The Letter of Peter to Philip (NHC VIII, 2)
Eug	The Letter of Eugnostos (NHC III, 3)
EV	(*Evangelium Veritatis*) The Gospel of Truth (NHC I, 3)
EvEg	The Gospel of the Egyptians (NHC III, 2)

EvPhil	The Gospel of Philip (NHC II, 3)
EvThom	The Gospel of Thomas (NHC II, 2)
ExAn	The Exegesis on the Soul (NHC II, 6)
ExpVal	A Valentinian Exposition (NHC XI, 2)
HA	The Hypostasis (= the Being) of the Archons (NHC II, 4)
Hyps	Hypsiphrone (NHC XI, 4)
Inter	The Interpretation of Knowledge (NHC XI, 1)
LibThom	The Book of Thomas (NHC II, 7)
2LogSeth	The Second Logos of the Great Seth (NHC VII, 2)
Mars	Marsanes (NHC X, 1)
Melch	Melchizedek (NHC IX, I)
Noema	The Concept of Our Great Power (NHC VI, 4)
OdNor	The Ode on Norea (NHC IX, 2)
OgdEnn	(*De Ogdoade et Enneade*) On the Eighth and the Ninth (NHC VI, 6)
OW	The Origin of the World (The Writing without a Title) (NHC II, 5)
PrecHerm	Hermetic Prayer (NHC VI, 7)
PrecPl	The Prayer of the Apostle Paul (NHC I, 1)
ParShem	The Paraphrase of Shem (NHC VII, 1)
Protennoia	The Trimorphic Protennoia (NHC XIII, 1)
Rheg	The Letter to Rheginus on the Resurrection (NHC I, 4)
Sextus	The Sentences of Sextus (NHC XII, 1)
Silv	The Teachings of Silvanus (NHC VII, 4)
SJC	The Sophia of Jesus Christ (NHC III, 4)
StelSeth	The Three Steles of Seth (NHC VII, 5)
TestVer	(*Testimonium Veritatis*) The Testimony of Truth (NHC IX, 3)
TractTrip	(*Tractatus Tripartitus*) The Tripartite Tractate (NHC I, 5)
Zostr	Zostrianos (NHC VIII, 1)

Bibliography

J. Lindsay, *The Origins of Alchemy in Greco–Roman Egypt*, 1970, 260–77, provides information about Ouroboros, the dragon eating its tail.

F. Siegert (*Zeitschrift für die neutestamentliche Wissenschaft* 71, 1980, 129–132) collects 'self–designations of the Gnostics in the Nag–Hammadi texts'; B. Layton, 'Prolegomena to the Study of Gnosticism', in L. M. White and L. Yarbrough (eds), *The Social World of the First Christians. Essays in Honour of W. A. Meeks*, 1995, 334–50, has most recently dealt with the terms 'gnosis' and 'Gnostic'. I myself have made an extensive analysis of the proposal worked out by the Congress of Messina in 1966, C. Markschies, 'Christliche Religionsphilosophie oder vorchristliche antike Religion: Was ist Gnosis?', in A. Franz (ed), *Glaube – Erkenntnis – Freiheit. Herausforderungen der Gnosis in Geschichte und Gegenwart*, 1999, 47–71. The monograph by M. A. Williams, *Rethinking 'Gnosticism'. An Argument for Dismantling a Dubious Category*, [2]1999, contains provocative and stimulating ideas.

For the topic of gnosis and the New Testament and the question of the history-of-religions derivation of the phenomenon, R. McL. Wilson, *Gnosis and the New Testament*, 1968, provides a guide along traditional lines; E. M. Yamauchi, *Pre-Christian Gnosticism. A Survey of the Proposed Evidences*, [2]1983, is rather more pointed and fresher. **R. Reitzenstein** (with **H. H. Schaeder**), *Das iranische Erlösungsmysterium. Religionsgeschichtliche Untersuchungen*, 1921, and **W. Bousset**, *Hauptprobleme der Gnosis*, 1973 (= 1907) or id., *Kyrios Christos. A History of the Belief in Christ from the Beginnings of Christianity to Irenaeus* (1921), 1970, are relevant to the classical theses of the 'history-of-religions school'; these are refuted by **C. Colpe**, *Die religionsgeschichtliche Schule. Darstellung und Kritik ihres Bildes vom gnostischen Erlösermythus*, 1961, and **H.-M. Schenke**, *Der Gott 'Mensch' in der Gnosis. Ein religionsgeschichtlicher Beitrag zur Diskussion über die paulinische Anschauung von der Kirche als Leib Christi*, 1962.

The relations between ancient 'gnosis' and modern theological schemes are investigated by the contributions to a composite volume edited by **P. Koslowski**, *Gnosis und Mystik in der Geschichte der Philosophie*, 1988 (which discusses, among others, Fichte, Schelling, Steiner and Jung). The text of the present book refers above all to **F. C. Baur**, *Die christliche Gnosis oder die christliche Religions-Philosophie in ihrer geschichtlichen Entwicklung*, 1835, and id., *Das Manichäische Religionssystems nach den Quellen neu untersucht und dargestellt*, 1928 (= 1831); **J. G. Fichte**, *Die Grundzüge des gegenwärtigen Zeitalters*, new edition by **F. Medicus**, 1943 (with the original 1806 pagination, which is cited); extracts from other basic scholarly positions on the topic are collected in **K. Rudolph** (ed), *Gnosis und Gnostizismus*, 1975. Special reference should be made to **H. Jonas**, *The Gnostic Religion*, [2]1991. Two major congresses on gnosis are documented by composite volumes: *Le origini dello gnosticismo. Colloquio di Messina 13–18 aprile 1966. Testi e discussioni pubblicati di U. Bianchi, 1967; The Rediscovery of Gnosticism. Proceedings of the International Conference on Gnosticism at Yale, New Haven, Connecticut, March 28–31, 1978*, ed **B. Layton** (2 vols), 1980.

The articles in the *Lexikon der antiken christlichen Denker*, ed **S. Döpp and W. Geerlings**, 1998 give admirable information about the Christian theologians mentioned in the section on sources, their biography, their works and their specific positions (they also contain information about the critical editions of the works mentioned and available German translations). The texts of the Arabic polymath al-Bīrūnī are most easily accessible in a selected edition by **G. Strohmaier**, Al-Bīrūnī, *In den Garten der Wissenschaft. Ausgewählte Texte aus den Werken des muslimischen Universalgelehrten*, 1988. Their value as sources was discussed by **C. Colpe** in his dissertation, *Der Manichäismus in der arabischen Überlieferung*, Göttingen 1954, which unfortunately is unpublished.

The writings of the Codices Askewianus and Brucianus, above all the so-called 'Pistis Sophia' and the 'Books of Jeû', are quoted according to the pagination and line numbering of the translation by **C. Schmidt** and **H.-M. Schenke**, *Koptisch–gnostische Schriften* 1 (Die Griechischen Christlichen Schriftsteller), ⁴1981; there is an English translation in the series Nag Hammadi Studies by **V. MacDermot** (NHS 9/13, 1978).

The present state of Nag Hammadi research and its history is best documented in a volume which appeared in 1997: *The Nag Hammadi Library after Fifty Years. Proceedings of the 1995 Society of Biblical Literature Commemoration*, ed **J. D. Turner** and **A. M. McGuire**, 1997. **A. Böhlig** and **C. Markschies**, *Gnosis und Manichäismus. Forschungen und Studien zu Valentin und Mani sowie zu den Bibliotheken von Nag Hammadi und Medinet Madi*, 1994, also gives a survey of the library. **J. M. Robinson**, *The Nag Hammadi Codices. A General Introduction to the Nature and Significance of the Coptic Gnostic Library from Nag Hammadi*, 1977, gives extensive information about the history of the find on the basis of his own researches, with abundant illustrative material; there is a brief account in **K. Rudolph**, *Gnosis*, 1987. The letters and business papers of monks from the cartonage of leather covers have been published in an edition by **J. W. Barns**, **G. M. Browne** and **J. C. Shelton**, *Greek and Coptic Papyri from the Cartonage of the Covers*, 1981.

The Coptic writings of the Nag Hammadi Library – which here are quoted by the original pagination of the Coptic pages – are published in three major critical editions: the American is almost complete, while the

French and German series have still to be completed. In addition there is also the great facsimile edition: *The Facsimile Edition of the Nag Hammadi Codices*, published under the auspices of the Department of Antiquities of the Arab Republic of Egypt in conjunction with the United Nations Educational, Scientific and Cultural Organization, with an introduction by **J. M. Robinson**, 12 vols, 1972–84. The American edition appeared with a translation in the series Nag Hammadi Studies, which at the same time, as an international archive, has also published investigations into the literature and what is so far a two-volume *Bibliographia Gnostica* by **D. M. Scholer**, *Nag Hammadi Bibliography 1948–69*, 1971; *Vol. 2, 1970–94*, 1997. This survey has since been continued in the journal *Novum Testamentum* and will in due course be collected again in a volume in the series Nag Hammadi and Manichaean Studies. The American series includes a compact edition which contains only translations and brief introductions: *The Nag Hammadi Library in English*, ed **J. M. Robinson**, [3]1988. The French series, Bibliothèque Copte de Nag Hammadi, publishes in a section entitled 'Textes' editions with a French translation and a full commentary, along with studies (section 'Études') and valuable concordances (section 'Concordances'). An edition of the writings of the Codices Askewianus and Brucianus has appeared in the *Griechische Christliche Schriftsteller*, edited by the Berlin-Brandenburgische Akademie der Wissenschaften (GCS Koptisch-Gnostische Schriften 1, [4]1981), as has a two-volume translation of the Nag Hammadi texts (GCS Koptisch-Gnostische Schriften II/III, 2001/2003). There is a whole series of Nag Hammadi texts in a critical edition with a translation and sometimes full commentary in the related series Texte und Untersuchungen; this series is being continued. There is an extensive bibliography of all editions of texts in the volume mentioned above edited by **A. Böhlig** and **C. Markschies**, *Gnosis und Manichäismus*, 225–42, but this only goes up to 1994. There is likewise a provisional dictionary with concordance: *Nag-Hammadi-Register. Wörterbuch zur Erfassung der Begriffe in* *den koptisch-gnostischen Schriften von Nag Hammadi*, prepared by **F. Siegert**, 1982. **C. Schmidt** and **H. J. Polotsky**, 'Ein Mani-Fund in Agypten. Originalschriften des Mani und seiner Schüler', *Sitzungsberichte der Preussischen Akademie der Wissenschaften. Philosophisch–historische Klasse*, 1933, 4–90, provides information about the discovery of the Medinet Madi library. Parts of the find in critical editions with a German translation appeared even before the Second World War, including **H. J. Polotsky**, *Manichäische Homilien*, 1934. The Dublin part is now accessible in a facsimile: **S. Giversen**, *The Manichaean Coptic Papyri in the Chester Beatty Library* (4 vols), Geneva 1986–8. The discovery of texts in China is best explored through two composite volumes with translations and brief commentaries: *Chinesische Manichaica, mit textkritischen Anmerkungen und einem Glossar*, edited and translated by **H. Schmidt-Glintzer**, 1987, and *Hymnen und Gebete der Religion des Lichts. Iranische und Türkische Texte der Manichäer Zentral-Asiens*, with an introduction and translation by **H.-J. Klimkeit**, expanded as *Gnosis on the Silk Road. Gnostic Texts from Central Asia. Gnosic Parables, Hymns and Prayers translated and presented by H.-J. Klimkeit*, 1993. In recent years some texts have appeared in good new editions within the framework of a major new project to produce editions of sources under the title Corpus Fontium Manichaeorum: *Die Bema-Psalmen*, ed **G. Wurst**, 1996, and *Die Herakleides-Psalmen*, ed **S. G. Richter**, 1998. The subsidiary series to the corpus includes a bibliography and the first volume of a lexicon: *Bibliographia Manichaica*, ed **G. B. Mikkelsen**, 1997, and *Dictionary of Manichaean Texts, Vol. 1, Texts from the Roman Empire*, 1998. **L. Koenen** and **C. Römer** have produced a critical edition with a German translation of the Cologne Mani Codex on the basis of the first edition of **A. Henrichs** and **L. Koenen**: *Der Kölner Mani-Kodex. Über das Werden seines Leibes*, 1988. For the state of research into the Manichaean texts generally see **A. Böhlig**, 'Neue Initiativen zur Erschliessung der koptisch-manichäischen Bibliothek von Medinet Madi', *Zeitschrift für die Neutestamentliche Wissenschaft* 80, 1989, 240–62; for the

138   *Gnosis: An Introduction*

new discoveries from the Dakhleh oasis cf. **I. Gardner**, 'The Manichaean Community at Kellis'. Progress Report', *Manichaean Studies Newsletter* 11, 1993, 18–26, and id., 'A Manichaean Liturgical Codex found at Kellis', *Orientalia* 62, 1993, 320–59. The texts discovered have been published in the 'Dakhleh Oasis Project', by Oxbow Books in Oxford: *Kellis Literary Texts*, Vol. 1, ed **I. Gardner**, 1996.

There is an excellent new German translation of the writings of the Corpus Hermeticum with a brief commentary: *Das Corpus Hermeticum Deutsch. Übersetzung, Darstellung und Kommentierung in drei Teilen*, edited for the Heidelberg Akademie der Wissenschaften by **C. Colpe** and **J. Holzhausen**, 1997; the older English translation by **W. Scott**, *Hermetica* (4 vols), 1924–26 (= 1987) is philologically highly problematical.

The Hekhalot literature has been made available above all by the publications of Peter Schäfer: *Synopse zur Hekhalot-Literatur*, ed **P. Schäfer**, 1981; there is a German translation of the Hekhalot literature in 4 vols edited by **P. Schäfer** and **K. Herrmann**, 1987–95; for a discussion of the theses of **G. Scholem**, *Major Trends in Jewish Mysticism*, 1995, cf. **P. Schäfer**, *Hekhalot-Studien*, 1988.

The description of the situation of early Christianity at the time of the Roman empire, which is only hinted at in the chapter on 'Early Forms of Gnosis', is developed in more detail in **C. Markschies**, *Between Two Worlds. Structures of Earliest Chrisitanity*, 1999. The fragments of Basilides are quoted according to **W. A. Löhr**, *Basilides und seine Schule. Eine Studie zur Theologie und Kirchengeschichte des zweiten Jahrhunderts*, 1996; the fragments of Valentinus according to **C. Markschies**, *Valentinus Gnosticus? Untersuchungen zur valentinianischen Gnosis mit einem Kommentar zu den Fragmenten Valentins*, 1992. **A. Hilgenfeld**, *Die Ketzergeschichte des Urchristentums*, 1963 (= 1884), is a fundamental analysis of the reports of early Christian theologians on Gnostics which has yet to be surpassed; **Simone Pétrement** has written a stimulating outside view: *A Separate God. The Christian Origins of Gnosticism*, 1990.

In addition to the editions of sources mentioned above, three studies by **S. N. Lieu** are particularly relevant to Manichaeism: *Manichaeism in the Later Roman Empire and Mediaeval China*, [2]1992; id., *Manichaeism in Mesopotamia and the Roman East*, 1994; id, *Manichaeism in Central Asia and China*, 1998.

Chronological Table

(*with* works [++ = lost; + = surviving only as a fragment]
and approximate dates of composition)

Early representatives of 'gnosis' ...	and their opponents in the church
Basilides (Alexandria, *c.*117–161): + *Exposition of the Bible*, 24 books	Justin (lived in Rome 150/155) ++ *Compendium against the Heretics*
Marcion (*c.*140 in Rome, died 160?) + *Antitheses*	Irenaeus of Lyons (*c.*180/185): *Refutation*
Valentinus (*c.*140 in Rome) + sermons, letters, psalms	
so–called pupils of Valentinus:	

– Ptolemy (Rome, second
century):
  Letter to Flora, outline of a
  system (?)	

– Theodotus + [title unknown]	Clement of Alexandria (*c.* 202–210) *Carpets, Excerpts from Theodotus*
– Heracleon (Italy, second century) + [exegetical] *Memorabilia*	Origen (Caesarea, Palestine, 232–48) + *Commentary on the Gospel of John*
	Tertullian (Carthage, 200–207ff.) *Indictment against the Heretics, Against the Valentinians, Against Marcion*

Later 'gnostics' and gnostic writings

Gnostic library of Nag Hammadi:
13 codices with around 50 writings,
including:
Gospels of Thomas, Philip and the
Egyptians [Nag Hammadi Codex II,
2 and 3; III, 3/IV, 2]
and non–Gnostic writings, e.g. Plato,
Republic 588a=589b [NHC VI, 5]

Codices Askewianus and Brucianus:
'Pistis Sophia', 2 'Books of Jeû'

Papyrus Berolinensis 8502:
Gospel of Mary, Secret Writing of
John [also NHC II, 1/III, 1/IV, 1],
Wisdom of Jesus Christ (NHC III, 4]

Mani (Persia, 216–276)
++ Extensive works of his own,
picture book, handbook, psalms of
the disciples

**Pagan philosophers also wrote
against the gnostics, thus above all:**

Hippolytus of Rome (c. 230?):
Refutation

Epiphanius of Salamis (374–7):
Medicine Chest

Augustine of Hippo (Africa,
378–421):
various writings, including *Against
Faustus*

Celsus (Alexandria, *c.*178):
+ *True Word*

Plotinus (Rome, 265):
Against the Gnostics

Index of Names

al-Bīrūnī 39
Alexander of Aphrodisias 2
Allbery, Charles Robert Cecil 61
Antony of Egypt 50
Aristotle 2, 32, 85
Augustine of Hippo 22, 39, 76, 105, 108, 117, 122, 142

Basilides 10, 79–81, 82, 83, 87, 89, 90, 99, 103, 121, 141
Bauer, Ferdinand Christian 11, 18, 22
Beatty, Alfred Chester 60
Berger, Klaus 65
Bethge, Hans-Gebhard 51
Blumenberg, Hans 121
Böhlig, Alexander 51
Bousset, Wilhelm 24, 25
Bultmann, Rudolf 71

Carpocrates 82

Celsus 7, 9, 142
Cerinthus 82
Clement of Alexandria 8, 9, 31–2, 36, 54, 56, 80, 141
Colorbasus 32
Colpe, Carsten 26

Doresse, Jean 48, 49

Epiphanius of Salamis 34–6, 89, 94, 96, 97, 98, 109, 112, 113, 115, 142
Ephraem 38
Eusebius 79

Fichte, Johann Gottlieb 12
Friedländer, Moriz 68

Giversen, Sören 61

Harnack, Adolf von 20
Hegel, G. W. F. 11, 12
Heracleon 32, 33, 71, 141

143